The NLP Activist

Richard Bolstad

The NLP Activist

The process of social transformation depends on skills that can be learned. You and your group can become more successful at creating the change you want. Your activism can enhance your sense of personal fulfillment instead of draining it. This book makes leading edge skills from the personal development and conflict resolution fields available for those seeking to assist successful political change at the grassroots level. In working with numerous political change organizations over the years, and training workers from groups such as Greenpeace New Zealand and the New Zealand Peace Foundation, I have an increasing sense of the importance of sharing the NLP skills for personal resilience and conflict management. This book is the outcome of 45 years of political activism and 40 years teaching communication skills.

Richard Bolstad is a certified trainer with the International Association for NLP. He teaches to government and educational managers, business groups, political activist organisations and coaches. Richard is a trained teacher, psychotherapist and a registered nurse and has been involved in political change movements for over 45 years. His books are available in many languages, and he teaches these skills in Asia, The Middle East, Australasia, the Americas and Europe.

The NLP Activist

Contents

NLP and Social Change 9

Goalsetting 13

Social Change Styles and Rapport 35

Reframing 48

Anchoring 56

Creating Relationships That Survive 67

How Do Activists *Influence* Society? 81

Creating a Campaign 104

Summary 107

Bibliography 110

Richard Bolstad

Dedication

To my grandson Leo. May he live in a better world than the one I grew up in. May he help create an even better one.

NLP and Social Change

Putting Alternative Psychology At The Service Of Social Change

This book is based on the belief that making the world a place worth living in deserves to be an enjoyable task. Social change agents have just as much right to the most advanced tools of twenty first century psychology as traditional professionals do. I think of this book as part of a project to share my own professional skills with the social change movements I am enthusiastic about.

My sense of the need for these skills comes from my work over 45 years in the peace movement, in organizations working to stop men's violence against women, in the anti-racism movement, in "revolutionary" anarchist groups and earlier in my life in the movement for democratic high schools. In the last decades I have trained people around the world working in social crisis situations, including, in my home country of New Zealand, workers from the New Zealand Peace Foundation and from Greenpeace New Zealand.

Social Change organizer and theorist Bill Moyer warns that "The culture of social movements often includes a sense of powerlessness, despair and failure that is consistent with – and sometimes produces – the "logical reasons" for believing that the movement is failing" (Moyer, 2001, p 91). Noam Chomsky echoes Moyer's concern and points out that the immediate origins of this culture of despair are not in the social environment but in the psychological responses of activists. "I mean, look; if you want to feel hopeless, there are a lot of things you could feel hopeless about.... First of all, those predictions don't mean anything – they're more just a reflection of your mood or your personality than anything else. And if you act on that assumption, then you're guaranteeing that'll happen. If you act on the assumption that things can change, well, maybe they will. Okay, the rational choice, given those alternatives, is to forget the pessimism." (Chomsky, 2002, p 139).

It's a great idea to "forget the pessimism" but how do you do it? Many social change activists are virtually traumatised by their experiences in the movement, and "burn out" is a more common reason for leaving this work than is a change of political viewpoint. In this article I want to present some answers from the field of Neuro Linguistic Programming (NLP). NLP is the psychology of how people use the human brain to achieve results in their own life, as well as to influence others and create social change. NLP can, I maintain, deliver us not only researched techniques for ending pessimism, but also new insights about how to achieve change in others.

From its beginnings, NLP has refused to accept the limitations and pessimism of traditional psychology. NLP has produced a number of one session change techniques with applications in accelerated learning, healing psychological trauma, physical health care, sports and elsewhere. To give a small example, in the years following the 1992-1995 Bosnian war, and during the attacks of Kosovo, I ran training for aid workers and psychiatrists in Sarajevo. I taught them one core NLP application; a twenty minute process for resolving Post Traumatic Stress Disorder (PTSD: the flashbacks, nightmares and panic attacks that frequently follow both natural and human-engineered disasters). Over ¾ of the psychiatrists I trained said they would immediately begin using the method, because it delivered better results than the longer "desensitisation" techniques of traditional psychology, and better results than anti-anxiety drugs (neither of which Bosnia-Herzegovina could then afford).

The Roots Of NLP

What are the philosophical roots of NLP? John Grinder, previously employed as an interpreter in the US Army, was a professor of Noam Chomsky's new science of Linguistics, and an organizer of anti-Vietnam war marches, at the time he and his student Richard Bandler co-developed NLP in the early 1970s (McClendon, 1989, p 35-36). "*Neuro Linguistics*" itself, however, is a term first coined by Alfred Korzybski as far back as 1933 (Korzybski, 1994, p lxxxix), to describe the science which would study the effects of language on the human brain. Korzybski warned then "At present the totalitarians have exploited neuro-semantic and neuro-linguistic mechanisms to their destructive limit." He urged that progressive groups would benefit from studying neuro-linguistics, suggesting that "For example, if consulted, such a body... would have studied *Mein Kampf* and various speeches of Hitler, Goebbels, etc, as a part of their duties, long ago, and would have advised their governments that psychopathological people are getting in control of world affairs and that their words cannot be trusted at all." This concern of Korzybski's must all have seemed a little paranoid in 1933 of course!

Alfred Korzybski set up the Institute of General Semantics to continue his work. The Editor of the Institute of General Semantics newsletter, Homer Jean Moore Junior noted almost immediately after September 11th 2001 that Korzybski would have been equally alarmed at President Bush's language and behaviour in September 2001, and that Korzybski would see immediately the links back to Goebbels and Hitler. Moore pointed out "In my life, the need for Korzybski's formulations has never been clearer." (Moore, 2001).

Korzybski's work analyzed the effects of language on the brain. He recognized that this knowledge could enable us not only to unpack propaganda, but also to construct useful messages to enable someone to change the way their brain operated. It was forty years before NLP began to tap this second potential of the neuro-linguistic link. In the 1970s a group of students and staff at the University of California in Santa Cruz began developing NLP as a method of understanding how change agents enable others to alter their lives in a positive direction. The group included John Grinder, Richard Bandler, Leslie Cameron, Judith Delozier and Robert Dilts. The first change agents they studied included Virginia Satir, a developer of Family Therapy, Fritz Perls, founder of Gestalt Therapy, and Milton Erickson a medical hypnotherapist. They studied Erickson, for example, not merely to know how to do "hypnotherapy", but to know how a hypnotherapist influences another positively, merely by talking to them. The results of this "modeling" can then be applied to any field where we want to have a positive influence on others. The number of NLP Practitioners world-wide is now in the hundreds of thousands.

NLP For Social Activists

Like any new discovery, NLP has been accessed most immediately by those in charge of the current status quo. For example, President Bill Clinton hired former NLP trainer Tony Robbins to advise him, and many of the world's most powerful multinational companies train their sales staff, public relations staff and management in NLP. The same situation occurred in the 1970s as new skills for creating group consensus emerged from the psychological "Encounter Movement". The new skills were quickly grabbed by "Organisational development" experts for use in business. Activist groups such as Movement For A New Society were at the forefront of reclaiming and integrating those new insights for the social change arena. Their work finally ended the era when radical groups were automatically run with all the democratic skill of Attila the Hun (Coover, Deacon, Esser, and Moore, 1978).

My aim here is similar. I want to provide some specific tools for us to use in social change movements. Of the thousands of NLP "techniques" and "models" which continue to be developed, my aim is to keep it simple by introducing five:

11

- **Goalsetting** (Let go of "problems" and "failure" based thinking and set goals that are worth achieving. Systematically set goals in the way that the most successful activists do.)
- **Rapport** (Understand and work with the personality differences that create the culture of a social change group, and the personality differences of the people you are trying to influence. Quickly create the feeling of shared understanding with another person enabling creative group solutions to be developed)
- **Reframing** (Detect and change hidden assumptions and "mind-fucks" in your own and others' language. Find the most useful meanings to events so as to detect new opportunities and get the most from "challenges")
- **Anchoring** (Instantly step into the state of mind to be able to easily do what you want to do: energised, enthusiastic, playful, inspired etc)
- **Cooperation** (Create supportive group relationships, negotiate successfully both inside your group and with those who oppose you)

I'm choosing these five tools as examples. There is much more to NLP that would benefit people in social change movements. For example, every year over 100 American protestors die from their allergic response to pepper spray (Yuen, Burton-Rose, and Katsiaficas, 2004, p 55); a response that can be resolved with a simple ten minute NLP Allergy response process (Swack, 1992). The twenty minute NLP Trauma reconsolidation process would be of enormous benefit to those whose experiences with the current social system have been violent or profoundly disturbing (Muss, 1991), and would also help explain the irrational phobic responses of millions of Americans to the events of September 11th 2001. But while these techniques do not require full professional training, they require at least a weekend workshop to get proficient with. I chose the above five topics because I want to give you skills you can take away from this book and use immediately to move beyond the pessimism and dramatically increase your effectiveness as a social change agent!

Goalsetting

How Goalsetting works

It's an often quoted saying that "If you don't know where you're going, you'll probably wind up somewhere else." The research confirms that the most successful people do indeed take more care working out where they are going. In their study of *Women of Influence* throughout history, Pat and Ruth Williams say that "The successful woman is the average woman, focused. The successful women in this book focused their lives.... They had a mission and they followed through." (Williams and Williams, 2003, p xvii).Edwin Locke and Gary Latham (1990) have surveyed 400 studies of goalsetting, showing that specific goals are the key to high success in fields as diverse as education, group management, sport and new year's resolutions. In a long term study of 250 students age 12-15, researchers Judith Meece, Allan Wigfield and Jacquelynne Eccles showed that the best predictor of whether students succeed is not how good they actually are but how good they *expect* to be in future (Meece Wigfield and Eccles, 1990). It is goals, not intelligence or skill, that determine success.

The history of every successful movement for social change is also the history of people willing to set goals and focus on them. In 1894, a year after leading the triumphant struggle for women's suffrage in New Zealand, Kate Sheppard was asked why she thought the women of England had not succeeded as had her own movement. People wondered what was different about the social situation in England. Sheppard replied "Is it because of vested interests which tend directly and indirectly to demoralisation?... or is it because women have not had the courage of their convictions and asked boldly for their rightful privileges, or know the reason why they have not got them?" Did Kate Sheppard understand the power of goal-setting? Absolutely. Her ability to "ask boldly" for what she wanted and identify what to adjust when she didn't get it was a key to the success of her movement. For Sheppard this meant putting aside her earlier work advocating alcohol prohibition. She realised that linking the women's suffrage movement to the movement to ban alcohol was losing support for her primary goal.

Over the 1920s and 1930s, the people of Samoa engaged in a courageous resistance to New Zealand police rule. In 1929 the leader of the Samoan "Mau" freedom movement (King Tamasese I) and others were shot dead by New Zealand police at a peaceful demonstration. Yet the Mau continued until its final success in 1962 when Samoa was granted independence. Tamasese's son (Tupua Tamasese Lealofi IV) became head of state and

Prime Minister. Did the Mau use goalsetting? Certainly. Their letter to the New Zealand administration after the death of Tamasese confirms it. At a time when they could have focused on their anger and grief, they focus instead on their core goal. "Samoa has drunk the shed blood of Tamasese and chiefs and orators and her beloved sons because we are looking forward to receiving for Samoa prosperity and liberty peacefully and without further suffering than has been endured up to the present time. No doubt it is the belief of Samoans that the day will soon dawn when the sun of righteousness will shine forth in Samoa." (Field, 1984).

In 1863 the New Zealand government "confiscated" three million acres of prime farming land from tribes who, led by the Maori king Tawhiao, had refused to sell it. The struggle to obtain some compensation was to span over four generations. It was King Tawhiao's grand-daughter, Princess Te Puea, who witnessed in 1947 the final acknowledgement by the government that the land had been stolen, and the gradual beginning of repayment. Imagine running a court case that takes 100 years to get justice! Did Tawhiao and Te Puea understand the ultimate success formula? Totally. A year after her success, Te Puea explained "... I have a programme of things to be done and only a limited time in which to do it .... It's no good looking backwards now. We've got be look to the future." Like Kate Sheppard, Te Puea recognised the need to focus attention on one specific goal. About campaigns to stop inter-cultural marriage, she said, "And that future has to include the Pakeha and Pakeha laws and even marriage to the Pakeha. We've simply got to strengthen our Maori roots so we can cope with it all and not stop being Maori." (King, 1977)

Setting Goals That Work For You

Richard Wiseman (2009, p 88-93) did a very large study of goalsetting. He tracked 5000 people who had some significant goal they wanted to achieve (everything from starting a new relationship to beginning a new career, from stopping smoking to gaining a qualification). He followed people up over the next year, and found firstly that only 10% ever achieved their goal. It wasn't just bad luck. Dramatic and consistent differences in the psychological techniques they used made those 10% stand out from the rest.

Those who failed tended either to think about all the bad things that would happen or continue to happen if they did not reach their goal (what NLP calls away from motivation, and what other research calls counterfactual thought) or to fantasise about achieving their goal and how great life would be if they somehow magically got what they wanted. They also tried to achieve their goal by willpower and by attempts to suppress "unhelpful thoughts". Finally, they spent time thinking about role models who had achieved their goal, often putting pictures of the role model on their fridge or other prominent places, to remind them to fantasise and wish they were like those people. Although the unsuccessful 90% were convinced that these strategies would help them, none of these techniques worked, and furthermore, the successful 10% did not waste their time doing these things.

The key to the problem 90% of us have lies in a series of complete misunderstandings about what a goal actually is. I am going to suggest that, mostly, the 90% failed because they did not actually have goals. In this chapter I want to distinguish goals from five completely separate cognitive structures: values, directions, problems, affirmations and competitive targets. All of these five structures may be useful, and using several of them at once is perfectly workable, but these last five are not goals. Starting "goal-setting" with one of the other structures in mind means not actually achieving the results that goal-setting promises.

Problems

The first thing that Wiseman found unsuccessful people did was to think a lot about how bad things have been for them, and how they are not where they want to be. Wiseman says "For example, when asked to list the benefits of getting a new job, successful participants might reflect on finding more fulfilling and well-paid employment, whereas their unsuccessful counterparts might focus on a failure leaving them trapped and unhappy." (Wiseman, 2009, p 92) Focusing on problems and what we don't want is paying attention to the past. It feels very different to focusing on the goal, outcome or solution to those problems, and it has very different, and less useful, results.

In 2000, Dr Denise Beike and Deirdre Slavik at the University of Arkansas conducted an interesting study of what they called "counterfactual" thoughts. These are thoughts about what has gone "wrong", along with what they could have done differently. Dr. Beike enlisted two groups of University of Arkansas students to record their thoughts each day in a diary in order to "look at counterfactual thoughts as they occur in people's day-to-day lives." In the first group, graduate students recorded their counterfactual thoughts, their mood, and their motivation to change their behaviour as a result of their thoughts. After recording two thoughts per day for 14 days, the students reported that negative thoughts depressed their mood but increased their motivation to change their behaviour. They believed that the negative thoughts were painful but would help them in the long term.

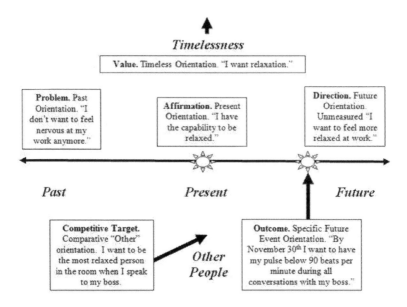

To test out this hope, the researchers then enlisted a group of students to keep similar diaries for 21 days, to determine if any actual change in behaviour would result from counterfactual thinking. Three weeks after completing their diaries the undergraduate students were asked to review their diary data and indicate whether their counterfactual thinking actually caused any change in behavior. "No self-perceived change in behaviour was noted," Dr. Beike told Reuters Health. Counterfactual thoughts about negative events in everyday life cause us to feel that we "should have done better or more," Dr. Beike said. "These thoughts make us feel bad, which motivates us to sit around and to feel sorry for ourselves." So what does work? The study found that "credit-taking thoughts", in which individuals reflect on success and congratulate themselves, serve to reinforce appropriate behavior and help people "feel more in control of themselves and their circumstances." (Slavik, 2003).

It is quite common, when working with a new client, for them to explain to me that their goal is "Not to be anxious". This contains no different information that the statement "My problem is being anxious". It does not tell me what they want instead. NLP Trainer Steve Andreas has a great metaphor for this. Imagine, he says, that you get into a taxi and tell the driver "I don't want to be here." And when the driver, in a puzzled way, says "Yes, but where do you wasn't to be instead of here?" you reply

"Well, somewhere else." There is no point in the driver moving her or his car until you learn to state a goal.

Values

The next most common response when I ask a new client about their goal, is for them to tell me a single word for a state of mind that they enjoy and value. "I want happiness." they say. In Wiseman's research, the most successful people were able to list concrete, specific benefits they would get from their goal, rather than just say that they would "feel happy". They had what Wiseman calls "an objective checklist of benefits" and made these "as concrete as possible", often by writing them down. He notes "… although many people said they aimed to enjoy life more, it was the successful people who explained how they intended to spend two evenings each week with friends and visit one new country each year." (Wiseman, 2009, p 91- 93). To explain the difference, if a client tells me that their goal is to be happy, I usually explain that there are pills that can do that for them easily. When they tell me they want to be happy without drugs, I tell them that avoiding all activity may be a really safe choice. Usually by that time they begin to get specific and explain exactly what they will be doing and thinking and how they will feel about that.

"Happiness" is not an end result, a goal. It is a state of being, a valued experience that could be experienced in many different contexts. To be able to check that they have achieved a goal, we need to know what the person's target context is, and what specific evidence they would need to know that they had achieved this desired state of being. A goal is not a value, it is a specific event which expresses or allows the expression of a value. Values are immensely useful to understand. Knowing a person's values enables them to check whether their goal will allow them to embody those values or not. Since values are what motivates a person to action, knowing them enables us to know whether they will actually want to achieve their goals or not (whether they will value those goals). A goalsetting process is like a ladder that a person climbs to reach what they want. A value is a wall that they would like to get to the top of. Leaning the ladder of goalsetting against the wrong wall means that the person is wasting their energy. But just choosing the right wall does not get you far in the process of climbing. Values tell you where it is worth going. Goals tell you how you will know you are taking steps in that direction.

Affirmations

Psychologists Joanne V. Wood and John W. Lee from the University of Waterloo, and W.Q. Elaine Perunovic from the University of New

Brunswick (Wood, Perunovic and Lee, 2009), first asked 249 research subjects to <u>fill in a short questionnaire</u> (the Rosenberg self-esteem scale) designed to analyse their self-esteem and to say how often they said positive things about themselves, on a scale from 1(never) to 8 (almost daily). 52% gave a rating of 6 or higher. These 52% of subjects, who already had high self-esteem, reported that they already often said affirming things to themselves. They reported using positive self-statements before exams (85%), before giving a presentation (78%), to cope with negative events (74%), and even sometimes as part of their everyday routine (23%). On average, they felt that such statements were helpful. Those with low self-esteem also claimed that such statements sometimes helped them, but they reported that affirmations more often made them feel worse. To find out why, the researchers did two follow-up studies.

First, they asked their subjects to write down anything they felt or thought in a four-minute period. The recruits included equal numbers of students with high or low self-esteem and half of each group were told to say to themselves, "I am a lovable person", every 15 seconds, on the cue of a bell rung by the researcher. Afterwards, they completed several questionnaires. Two of these were designed to assess their mood, including questions such as "What is the probability that a 30-year-old will be involved in a happy, loving romance?" and "Would you like to go to a party?" Another set of questions rated their current self-esteem by asking them to say which of two adjectives they felt closest to – e.g. valuable or useless, nice or awful, good or bad. As you might expect, the students with higher self-esteem had higher, happier scores on all three questionnaires than those with low self-esteem. After saying the affirmations, there was no statistically significant change in their scores. But for those subjects who already had low self-esteem, the effect of the affirmations was dramatic and negative. They felt worse after saying these words, had more negative beliefs, and had lower expectations of success. Their self-esteem scores were almost halved as a result of trying to use affirmations.

The researchers explain the result by saying that everyone has a range of ideas they are prepared to accept. Messages that lie within this boundary are more persuasive than those that fall outside it - those meet resistance and can even lead to people holding onto their original position more strongly. If a person with low self-esteem says something that's positive about themselves but is well outside the range of what they'll actually believe, their immediate reaction is to dismiss the claim and feel even worse. Statements that contradict a person's current self-image and basic model of the world, no matter how positive in intention, are likely to trigger mismatching thoughts.

Of course, as an NLP Practitioner, you have several interventions that can change self-image and model of the world so that these affirmations would work... and of course then the affirmations may not seem so important anyway. Wood concluded that affirmations only work in situations where people make very specific statements that are impossible to argue with, or where none of their major beliefs are challenged. For example, people may be better off saying "I choose good gifts for people" rather than "I'm a generous person". Put in the terms of my communication skills text Transforming Communication (Bolstad, 2002), positive statements are better worded as sensory specific "I messages" rather than as judgments. Wood and colleagues cautioned that "outlandish, unreasonably positive self-statements, such as "I accept myself completely," are often encouraged by self-help books. Our results suggest that such self-statements may harm the very people they are designed for: people low in self-esteem." (Wood, Perunovic and Lee, 2009, p 865)

In the third study, subjects were asked to consider the statement "I am a lovable person" and either to focus only on ways in which it's true, or to consider ways in which it is and isn't true. After the task, people with high self-esteem benefited from focusing only on the positive side of the statement, but those with low self-esteem felt worse about themselves if they dwelled only on positives, and better if they were asked to take a more balanced approach. Wood suggests that if people with low self-esteem are asked to think only positive thoughts, and find it difficult to block out negative ones, that merely certifies their belief that they aren't measuring up to standards.

NLP developers Richard Bandler and John Grinder did not include "affirmations" in their list of NLP techniques. Robert Dilts and Judith DeLozier in their Encyclopaedia of NLP (Dilts and DeLozier, 2000, p 24) do champion affirmations, saying "Affirmation is a method for creating, strengthening and encouraging positive 'self-fulfilling' processes. "Affirmation" essentially involves the verbal assertion and reinforcement of empowering beliefs. The process of affirmation involves the repetition of a series of belief statements. In many ways, affirmations represent a fundamental example of "neuro-linguistic programming". They employ the use of language to establish and encourage positive mental "programming"." However, Dilts and DeLozier's examples of affirmations are all current reality based. Put another way, Dilts and DeLozier's examples are all process oriented e.g. "It is possible for me to be healthy and well," "I have the capabilities to be healthy and well," rather than outcome based "I am healthy and well." The above research suggests that since their affirmations don't challenge the client's "reality" they are more likely to be received positively.

Bandler and Grinder did develop methods for transforming internal beliefs, and they seem to have been very aware of the risk of contradicting a person's experience of reality. Bandler, for example, describes creating a new belief as creating a new focus of attention, rather than contradicting the evidence that a person has collected about "reality". Describing the construction of new beliefs, Richard Bandler says (1985, p 105-109) "Do you know what belief you'd like to have in place of the belief you have now?... Start thinking about it now, and be sure you *think about it in positive terms*, not in terms of negations. Think of what you do want to believe, not what you don't want to believe. I also want you to frame that belief not in terms of an end or goal, but in terms of a *process* or *ability* that would result in you getting that goal. For instance if you'd like to believe that you know NLP, change it so that you believe you can pay attention, and learn and respond to feedback in order to learn NLP.... We want to mobilize new abilities, not install new delusions!" To the extent that "Every day in every way I am getting better and better," (to quote one traditional affirmation) is inconsistent with reality, it is of course a delusion. No wonder many people in the research resist it.

In relation to goals, what this research shows is that stating your goals (what you want to happen in the future) as affirmations (what you appreciate about what is happening now) is counterproductive. Affirming your current strengths, resources, achievements and gratitude is very useful, but it cannot replace goalsetting.

Although focusing on the problem you have had does not lead to success, neither does merely fantasising about the future success. Lien Pham and Shelley Taylor at the University of California did a study where a group of students were asked to visualise themselves getting high grades in a mid-term exam that was coming up soon. They were taught to form clear visual images and imagine how good it will feel, and to repeat this for several minutes each day. A control group was also followed up, and the study times of each student as well as their grades in the exam were monitored. The group who were visualising should, according to proponents of "The Secret" DVD and the "Law of Attraction", have a clear advantage. Actually, they did much less study, and consequently got much lower marks in the exam (Pham and Taylor, 1999).

This result is very consistent. There are now a large number of research studies showing that "The secret" or "The law of attraction" (visualising your outcome and then letting go and trusting that the universe will provide it) impedes success. Gabrielle Oettingen at the University of Pennsylvania has done a number of studies showing the same result. In one study, women in a weight-reduction program were asked to describe what would happen if they were offered a tempting situation with food. The more positive their fantasies of how well they would cope with these situations, the less work they did on weight reduction. A year later, those women who consistently fantasised positive results lost on average 12 kilos less than those who anticipated negative challenges and thus put in more effort (Oettingen and Wadden, 1991). Oettingen followed up final year students to find out how much they fantasised getting their dream job after leaving university. The students who fantasised more reported two years later that they did less searching for jobs, had fewer offers of jobs, and had significantly smaller salaries than their classmates (Oettingen and Mayer, 2002). In another study she investigated a group of students who had a secret romantic attraction, a crush, on another student. She asked them to imagine what would happen if they were to accidentally find themselves alone with that person. The more vivid and positive the fantasies they made, the less likely they were to take any action and to be any closer to a relationship with the person 5 months later. The result is consistent in career success, in love and attraction, and in dealing with addictions and health challenges (Oettingen, Pak and Schnetter, 2001; Oettingen, 2000; Oettingen and Gollwitzer, 2002).

Directions

The last two types of non-goal are at least moving in a useful direction. However they measure themselves not against a desired future success, but against some aspect of the present situation. As it implies, a direction only tells you the direction, and not how far the person wants to get to by a certain time. A person may say, I want to earn more money next year than this year (meaning that if they earn one cent more, their goal has been achieved) or I want to be more relaxed when talking to my boss (meaning that a pulse rate just 5 beats per minute below their current level of anxiety would be goal success). In some ways this is very valuable information. A positive "towards" motivated direction is a generative plan (i.e. it keeps generating new actions) rather than one that leads only to one specific point. Some people would benefit by having more direction, rather than only specific targets. In that sense, directions are similar to values; they give an ongoing check that you are doing something useful. They are not goals.

Competitive Targets

Imagine that a client tells you that their problem is that they want to remain relaxed while they talk with their boss (problem), and they value calmness (value), and they know they have the ability to relax (affirmation). Then they explain "So my goal is that when I am speaking to my boss, I will be the most relaxed person in the room." Probably, you would immediately identify that even if they can measure their bosses relaxation (and they need to be able to do so to know if they achieved this "goal", in order to check that they are even more relaxed than the boss) this "goal" has some unhelpful consequences.

Firstly, it divides their attention, because usually a person measures their own success. In this case they must measure both their own success and the success of the others in the room, and then effectively compare these. It divides their attention between the two competitors. Secondly, the goal is almost worthless, because technically they will still have achieved it if they find that they are (for example) fractionally less than the psychological mess that their boss is. They are setting a goal and allowing their bosses level of success to decide how much they will reach for. The same two problems occur with all competitive goals – being "the highest earning person in my business", having "a closer relationship than any of my family" etc. Given the obvious ineffectiveness of such competitive goals, why do new clients choose them?

The answer is a social mythology around the value of "Competition." The belief many parents, teachers and team leaders have is that trying to do better than someone else leads to success, and even "builds character." David and Roger Johnson (in Kohn, 1986, P47) reviewed 122 research studies on how co-operation or competition affect success. In only 8 of these studies did competition seem to help. In most of the studies, people co-operating were far more successful, and felt better about their achievement at the end. Airline pilots who are competing against each other fly less safely than those who co-operate. Scientists who are competing for honours make less scientific advances. A study of business people showed that the most successful business people were the least competitive, dramatically contradicting what was being taught in business training. John Simmons and William Mares (in Kohn, 1986, p213) review studies of co-operatively run workplaces showing that they produce more than hierarchical and competitive ones. The reason is very simple. Competition requires paying attention to how the other person is doing. Success requires paying attention to how you are doing. The competitor is like a person running a race while looking over their shoulder to check the others (a problem which actually obstructs even sports success, and feeds what is known as competitive anxiety, where the sportsperson can perform better in practice than in the actual sports "competition". If you want to succeed - personally and in your group - the answer is to focus on your own achievements.

Let me show you with a goal set by a man I'll call Kori. When Kori came to see me, he said "I want to set up an internet site to provide information about local social change meetings."

1. Sensory Specific:

Firstly, the most successful people in Wiseman's research did imagine achieving their goal, and were able to list concrete, specific benefits they would get from it, rather than just say that they would "feel happy". They had what Wiseman calls "an objective checklist of benefits" and made these "as concrete as possible", often by writing them down. He notes "… although many people said they aimed to enjoy life more, it was the successful people who explained how they intended to spend two evenings each week with friends and visit one new country each year." (Wiseman, 2009, p 91- 93)

First, I asked Kori, "Exactly when do you plan to have achieved that goal?" That kind of surprised him. Many people who don't know about NLP still think of change as a hit and miss affair. "Maybe in a year I'll be there, and probably it will all be pretty cool." kind of thing. Kori decided that "a month from now" would be better for timing. Next I told him "Step into your body a month from now, with this goal achieved. What do you see that's different, what do you hear, and what do you feel differently?" Just answering this question, imagining himself showing the new internet site to friends a month later, causes Kori to involve all his sensory systems (visual, auditory, kinesthetic etc) and thus to "engage" larger areas of his brain than if he simply thought through the words of his stated goal. Right away he said he felt more confident that it could happen.

In my personal experience, many political activities don't even get this far in the goalsetting process. Liza Featherstone, Doug Henwood and Christian Parenti express grave concern about the anti-intellectualism of the 2001-2003 anti-war movement. "So we want to stop the humanitarian crisis in Afghanistan – what does it mean to have that as our goal?" they question, pointing out that the peace movement dwindled when activists had no clear answer to questions about what an Afghanistan without a humanitarian crisis would look like - did they want the Taliban left to rule "in peace", for example? (Featherstone et alia, 2004, p 331).

2. Positive Language :

Secondly, in Wiseman's study, the successful people described their goal positively. Wiseman says "For example, when asked to list the benefits of

23

getting a new job, successful participants might reflect on finding more fulfilling and well-paid employment, whereas their unsuccessful counterparts might focus on a failure leaving them trapped and unhappy." (Wiseman, 2009, p 92)

One of the things Kori said would be different in his case was "I don't have that internal voice telling me I'm a failure." Often when people set a goal, they say what they *don't* want. In the brain this doesn't work so well. Here's how I explained it to him "Kori, let me show you something about how the brain works. *Don't* think of a blue tree. Got that? *Don't* think of a blue tree. Keep not thinking of a blue tree ..... Now, what are you thinking of." He laughed "A blue tree!"

"Right," I agreed. "If you want your brain to achieve your goal, the way to do it is to tell it what it *will* think of, not what it won't. If you tell it don't be a failure, in order to *understand* what you're saying it has to think about failing. To get it to *stop*, you tell it, *"Do* get the results you wanted.""

"Okay," he said, "My goal is to set up an internet site to provide information about local social change meetings. And when I think of it in sensory specific ways, I guess I hear my internal voice telling me how well I'm doing ... Wow, that's weird. That's a whole new experience."

In the current global movement, this change in terminology has been discussed already. One recent article urges, "The movement is also undergoing a fascinating rhetorical shift, as activists reject terms like "antiglobalization", which emphasised − not very lucidly − what they're against, in favour of slogans like "Another World Is Possible" which dare to evoke the possibility of radically different economic arrangements. What would that other world look like? Activists must engage that question." (Featherstone et alia, 2004, p. 314). These names require us to make very different "internal representations" (imagined pictures, sounds, words and body sensations) in order to think about them. The term "antiglobalization" is a little like the phrase "Don't think of a blue tree". It requires the speaker to make an internal representation of capitalist globalisation in order to understand it. The term "another world" generates a very different internal representation. This is why many people prefer the term "Peace movement" to "Anti-war movement".

Focusing on problems and what we don't want is tempting. It feels very different to focus on the goal, outcome or solution to those problems. As we noted above, studies show "credit-taking thoughts", in which individuals reflect on success and congratulate themselves, serve to reinforce appropriate behavior and help people "feel more in control of themselves and their circumstances." (Slavik, 2003).

Based on this understanding, psychotherapists Steve de Shazer, Insoo Kim Berg and others (Miller et alia, 1996) have developed a model of change called the Solution-Focused approach. The following are examples of their questions, which guide a group to identify what they want and how to get it:

- "If you solve this problem, what will you get as a result?"
- "What has to be different as a result of us meeting?"
- "What do we want to achieve?"
- "What would need to happen for us to feel that this problem was solved?"
- "How will we know that this problem is solved?"
- "When this problem is solved, what will we be doing and feeling instead of what we used to do and feel?"
- "How will this meeting will help us move towards our goals?"

3. Ecological:

But not all of goalsetting is based on thinking about the "ideal". For example, one surprising result of the research by both Gabrielle Oettingen and Richard Wiseman is that it pays to think about challenges you may face in achieving your goal (even though that may feel unpleasant at the time). After thinking about the positive benefits of achieving their goal, the most successful participants would "spend another few moments reflecting on the type of barriers and problems they are likely to encounter if they attempt to fulfil their ambition.... focusing on what they would do if they encountered the difficulty." (Wiseman, 2009, p 101) Oettingen trained people to do this process, which she calls "doublethink" and NLP would call checking "ecology". She was able to increase their success dramatically just with this step.

Is this new experience OK for all of you? That was what I wanted to check next in my work with Kori. What consequences that he might not have thought of could result if he changed. In Neuro Linguistic Programming (NLP) we call this being "ecological", using a metaphor from the consequences of environmental change. Before European settlement, 70 percent of New Zealand was covered in forest. Enthusiastic settlers with powerful goals (personal wealth, farming lifestyles, national prosperity etc) have reduced this percentage to 22. It's an impressive example of the power of a dream with a use by date. *And*, the biggest petition ever presented to New Zealand's parliament was the 1977 Maruia declaration: 341000 New Zealanders calling for a halt to the cutting of native forests. They represented the concern about *the consequences of reaching our goals*. It's the same with personal goals.

I asked Kori "What other things will change if you achieve this goal? Especially, what benefits do you get from not having the internet site, that might be at risk if you change?"

"Hmm", he nodded. "I guess feeling that I'm still only setting up the site means that I have an excuse for not getting more involved in the actual meetings. If I had achieved that, I might end up doing a lot more group work and things like that. That's OK; I just need to work out how much new involvement I can manage."

I nodded. "This may seem strange, but I think it's a useful question: Is there any situation in your life that you don't want to be affected by the results of this goal?"

He shook his head. "I don't think so. I guess the only thing would be that I don't want to be seen as the "Internet guy" and always be asked questions about the internet at meetings!"

"Okay. So that's two things about the consequences which you want to incorporate into your goal. You want to be seen as an activist and not a "computer geek", and also you'll be learning some new skills for dealing with the requests to get more involved. Is that right?" He nodded.

For social activists, assessing the ecology of our work (its implications for the rest of our lives) is crucial to avoid "burnout" and exhaustion. Noam Chomsky says "Look, you're not going to be effective as a political activist unless you have a satisfying life. I mean there *may* be people who are really saints but I've never heard of one. Like, it may be that the political activities themselves are so gratifying that they're all you want to do, and you just throw yourself into them. Okay, that's a perfectly fine thing to be – it's just that most people have other interests: they want to listen to music, they want to take a walk by the ocean, they want to watch the sunset. Any human being is too rich and complex just to be satisfied with these things, so you have to hit some kind of a balance." (Chomsky, 2002, p 354).

Another type of ecology issue arises from the effects of actions outside us. It often takes careful consideration to identify the consequences of social change. "Mohammed tried to be kindly and tolerant," say Stuart Christie and Albert Meltzer, "when he decreed that everyone who freed a slave would be certain of a place in Paradise. He did not forsee that his liberal reform would mean that slavery would linger on in Moslem countries long after it had become obsolescent elsewhere, for how else would the ruling-class assure its place in Paradise?" (Christie and Meltzer, 1972, p 117).

4. Choice Increases:

One way to describe what I'm checking with the questions about ecology is that the person's sense of choice increases with this goal. Some people have had the idea that change means getting rid of a bad choice. A person wanting to give up alcohol use may ask "How can I take away the choice of getting drunk?" for example." Instead, NLP maintains that real change means increasing good choices, so the person simply won't bother using the old one. "How can you find some new choices for relaxing and having fun with people that are so exciting that the idea of getting drunk just bores you?" The brain is designed to respond positively to new options or choices. It easily builds new neural networks to enable new types of action. It does not easily "cut out" old choices. Each new experience adds interconnections between the neurons; it does not reduce old connections. In goalsetting, we copy that strategy. "Flexibility" is a strong value of NLP.

I want to check that Kori is primarily adding a new choice, rather than avoiding old ones. He could always choose not to continue updating the internet site; he just has more options.

Part of the pessimism of social movements is related to the feeling of inevitability; the sense that we have no choice but to act in a certain way. The most successful movements are choice enhancing. About the ending of Apartheid, for example, Peter Ackerman and Jack Duvall explain "When it confronted the township revolt in 1984, the South African regime still wrongly saw apartheid's opponents as guerrilla warriors and it's own action as counter-revolutionary, so the blunderbuss of repression was its method. But when township activists organised rent strikes, work stay-aways, and consumer boycotts, when African township counsellors and police were condemned for cooperating with the government, and when street committees took over public functions such as sanitation and criminal justice, the movement was in too many places doing too many things for Pretoria's strategy of "taking out" key militants to work." (Ackerman and Duvall, 2000, p. 498). About the current world movement for global justice, Edie Yuen points out that "Since "flexibility" is rivalled only by "globalization" as a buzzword of neoliberalism, it is fitting that the tactics of the movement are as nimble as the flows of finance capital." (Yuen, 2004, p xii).

27

5. Initiated by Self:

Successful goal setters work out what *they'll* do different, not merely what everyone else ought to do. It's disempowering to set goals about what the government will do or what other activists will do, without identifying what you will do to enable that to happen. Kori can spend all day *wishing* that someone would pay him to set up the site. The question is, what will *he* do to start things changing.

Successful goal-setters have a plan. They do not leave their goal up to "the law of attraction" or to someone else who will save them. Wiseman notes "Whereas successful and unsuccessful participants might have stated that their aim was to find a new job, it was the successful people who quickly went on to describe how they intended to rewrite their CV in week one, and then apply for one new job every two weeks for the next six months." (Wiseman, 2009, p 91)

Eddie Yuen points out that one of the major causes of pessimism and powerlessness in social change movements is thinking in terms of the system changing, rather than in terms of the movement creating those changes. "There are two major reasons for this. The first is that Power (*"La Pouvre,"* as dissidents in Algeria so succinctly describe their system) will never credit oppositional forces with forcing them into concessions or defeats. The second is that the movement reinforces this narration by distaining the reformist or rhetorical victories it *actually* achieves, as its power stems from its uncompromising ambition to *radically* change the world. The resulting erasure of popular struggle from history has led many to believe that labor laws, civil rights, and environmental protections were all spontaneously granted by benevolent elites after thoughtful consideration." (Yuen, 2004, p. xxiv). Another frame which creates the same disempowerment is conspiracy theory, where social change activists become convinced that history is being shaped by a secret cabal of evil rulers. Yuen continues "The propensity to seek monocausal explanations leads to weak arguments that in turn may lure some activists to the safe havens of sectarian dogma or conspiracy theory…. History is neither made by great men nor "evil doers", and it is up to the movement to offer an alternative to the apocalyptic dualism that is engulfing the world." (Yuen, 2004, p. xxi)

6. First Step Identified and Achievable:

How many times have you heard a cigarette smoker tell you they'll give up next year? It's a great goal, but what they need are small, achievable steps along the way. When someone sets a goal, I always ask them "What small first step will you take *today*?" Kori might compile a list of all the current meetings that he wants to have on his site. He might email all the groups to ask for descriptions of their activities. He might investigate ten other sites which perform a similar function on the internet, for ideas. He might collect the graphics he wants to use. He might purchase the domain name that he will use for the site.

Wiseman found that it was particularly important to break the goal down into small steps and manage one step at a time. "Successful participants broke their overall goal into a series of sub-goals, and thereby created a step-by-step process that helped remove the fear and hesitation often associated with trying to achieve a major life change." (Wiseman, 2009, p 90-91)

Another cause of disempowering pessimism in social change movements is the all-or-nothing obsession with the "ultimate goal", the "end of history", the "great revolution". Introducing his MAP model, Bill Moyer restates "Social movements do not win overnight. Successful social movements typically progress through a series of eight clearly definable stages, in a process that often takes years or decades. The Movement Action Plan's Eight Stages Model enables activists to identify the particular stage their social movement has reached, celebrate successes achieved by completing previous stages, and create effective strategies, tactics, and programs for completing the current stage and moving to the next. As they follow this process, activists are able to develop strategies to achieve short-term goals that are part of the long-term evolution to their ultimate objective." (Moyer et alia, 2001, p. 42). The stages Moyer lists are:

1) The public is completely unaware of the contradiction between widely held positive values and the damaging results of the present system.
2) Opposition groups emerge and begin research to prove a problem exists, as well as attempting to use accepted channels of change to solve it.
3) Public recognition and concern about the problem grows and perhaps ¼ of the public understands the negative effects of current structures or policies.
4) Trigger events lead to dramatic non-violent campaigns that increasingly expose the injustice of present situations.
5) Numbers involved in the campaign drop as goals are not yet achieved. Frustration at failure provokes more destructive protests as well as the ongoing non-violent ones.

6) Retriggering events create majority support for the movement. Power structures present the movement's proposed solutions as dangerous for social stability.
7) Splits appear in the ranks of the powerholders about how to respond. Minimal reforms are rejected as the movement gains overwhelming support and new laws and institutions emerge.
8) The movement deals with backlash hostility by old powerholders, and new issues emerge from the new situation.

Successful activists seem to understand this cycle. Let me give an example. In 1891 the campaign to get New Zealand women the vote went to parliament. It was defeated by seventeen votes to fifteen in the legislative council. The movement's most well known activist Kate Sheppard, writing in the magazine of the suffrage movement could have said that this meant that all their work had failed. Instead she wrote "... our temporary defeat will have the effect of spurring on all who earnestly desire to see this reform carried, to greater zeal and energy, so that the majority favourable in the House of Representatives next session may be so large that the Legislative Council will not throw the Bill out again." (Devaliant, 1992, p 71). Sheppard had identified her movement successfully moving through Moyer's stage 5 while others had given in to the despair that this stage often generates.

7. Your Resources Identified :

As he thinks of each of the possibilities for a first step, what Kori is also doing is identifying the resources he has to change. These resources include :

♦   support systems: people who can give encouragement as well as resources (perhaps people from the groups that his site will promote).
♦   information sources (in this case, including the groups whose activities he will promote).
♦   time and money he has available to put into the above things.
♦   strategies that work for him in other situations where he wants to achieve something (ways of getting up in the morning, managing his time, inspiring himself and so on).
♦   role models (in this case developers of other internet sites focusing on social change) who have the skills he wants.

Before the 1992 UN ban on the use of driftnets on the high seas, hundreds of thousands of whales and dolphins died in these nets each year. Fishermen killed dolphins en masse because they believed that the dolphins competed for their catch, but spokespeople from the fishing industry consistently denied that the carnage was happening. When biologist Sam LaBudde learned about the dolphin slaughter, he determined to do whatever it took to stop the slaughter. The problem was that his personal resources seemed low, and no-one had been able to provide the documentary evidence to prove that there was a problem. A $35,000 film by Stan Minasian, shot in 1975, had barely had any public impact because of this lack of video evidence.

In 1988, Sam LaBudde spent $300, which was all the money he had, on a video camera. He drove across the border to Mexico and managed to get hired as a cook by the owner of a Panamanian fishing boat. Once aboard he surreptitiously videotaped the dolphin slaughter. LaBudde's footage provided the first graphic evidence that tuna fishermen were indiscriminately slaughtering dolphins. LaBudde testified before the United States Congress and the footage was shown on national television, provoking outrage across the country. In the months that followed, LaBudde worked with the Earth Island Institute and the Marine Mammal Fund to launch the most successful consumer boycott in U.S. history. By spring of 1990, the three major tuna brands agreed to process only dolphin-safe tuna, resulting in a 95 percent reduction in dolphin kills. Months later LaBudde returned to sea, this time to document open-ocean driftnetting, a destructive fishing method using nets 50 to 60 kilometers long. With this video footage, LaBudde led a campaign that resulted in a 1992 United Nations resolution banning the use of driftnets. (Wallace and Gancher, 1993, p. 37-60).

Sam LaBudde's story demonstrates his incredible creativity with the minimal external resources (eg money) he had. Notice that each step along the way to his goal becomes another type of resource. His sense of being able to achieve things, his sense of confidence that what he is doing can work, is building all the time. This sort of internal resource is even more important than the external finances and numbers of people involved, in determining success.

All Results Are Feedback

When you take action towards your goal, you'll always get results. You may not always get the result you expected, but you'll always get some result. If you pay attention to whether your result is what you wanted then you'll learn from any result. Lastly, you need the flexibility to do something different if you didn't get what you want.

There's no failure in this system. If a boat is sailing from Christchurch, New Zealand to Sydney, Australia and the captain discovers that winds have caused them to be heading for Brisbane, further north, what does she do? Does she decide that proves she's a failure and sink the boat? No way. She takes advantage of the feedback to reset her course. Thomas Edison invented 1093 different devices in his lifetime, including the electric light and the battery. In trying to find something that would store electricity in a battery, he unsuccessfully used around 10,000 substances. When a friend told him it must be hard to have failed so often, Edison explained "Why, I have not failed. I've just found 10,000 ways that won't work."

Bill Moyer points out that the failure model has been very powerful in the history of social change movements. He advocates celebrating successes and appreciating feedback. He says "For example, in 1982, stopping deployment of the Cruise and Pershing 2 nuclear missiles in Europe was the American peace movement's top goal. At the time, this goal seemed crucial, yet difficult to accomplish. Over the next few years, the movement adopted even bigger goals that were considered more important, including a freeze on building all nuclear weapons. When Reagan and Gorbachev signed the INF Treaty in 1986, ending the deployment of Cruise and Pershing 2 nuclear missiles in Europe, the American movement hardly noticed. The following day, one activist at the Nuclear Freeze office in San Francisco said to me, "What is there to celebrate? They are building five nuclear bombs a day."

Successful goal-setters celebrate results. Let me give you another example. Kate Dewes is a teacher from Christchurch, New Zealand. It was while viewing images from the Peace Museum at Hiroshima that Dewes set a goal which changed the course of her life. In 1979 she began to work with retired Christchurch magistrate Harold Evans and others on a scheme to have the United Nations International Court of Justice ("The World Court") declare nuclear weapons illegal. By 1991 she and her colleagues set up the World Court Project, with branches across the world. Their biggest problem was that only United Nations organisations and member states are able to take a case to the world court.

A breakthrough came after Dewes met with New Zealand doctors involved in International Physicians for the Prevention of Nuclear War (IPPNW). Together, Dewes, Dr Erich Geiringer and Dr Robin Bryant found a novel "way in" to the United Nations. They began urging governments to raise the matter as a health issue at the World Health Organisation. After a visit to the Ukrainian embassy in London, the Ukraine (where Chernobyl was stationed) agreed to support them. Other countries followed. At the World Health Organisation annual assembly in 1993, a resolution was proposed calling for the World Court to consider the legality of nuclear weapons. WHO voted in support by 73 votes to 40.

The WHO decision produced big enough ripples so that by the next year, the World Court Project got the agreement of the "Non-Aligned Movement" (a loose grouping of 111 of the United Nations' 185 member states). The issue was raised at the United Nations itself, and finally referred to the World Court. Behind the scenes, Kate's World Court Project was now running a huge campaign. It collected almost four million declarations of conscience in forty different languages, urging support for the project. It lobbied every government in the world, not only urging them to support the goal, but thanking them profusely whenever they did so. On July 8th, 1996, the International Court of Justice declared that the threat or use of nuclear weapons was "generally contrary to the rules of international law". The implications of this decision are enormous. Most of the world still does not realise what Kate Dewes and her friends have achieved. For example, under the principles defined by the United Nations during the Nuremberg trials of Nazi war criminals, it is correct for any citizen to oppose government action which breaches the rules of international law. (Dewes, 1998).

Kate Dewe's success depended on her ability to set a clear goal. Once she found that it was impossible for individuals to take cases to the world court, she didn't consider that failure. It was merely feedback to let her know what she needed to do next.

Interdependence: Virginia Satir's Example

One of the criticisms of goalsetting is that it focuses people only on their own resources, alienating them from the support of others. Returning to the roots of NLP, we have an excellent model of how to go beyond this, in the practice of Virginia Satir. The first NLP model (the metamodel) was developed by the study of Satir's work as a social worker in families (Grinder and Bandler, 1975). Satir gives a great example of working in a way respectful of peoples interdependence, rather than their separateness. "Some years ago I took on an assignment in a southern county to work with people on public welfare." She explains (Satir, 1993, p 204-206). "What I wanted to do was show that everybody has the capacity to be self-sufficient and all we have to do is to activate them. I asked the county to pick a group of people who were on public welfare, people from different racial groups and different family constellations. I would then see them as a group for three hours every Friday." Satir asked each person what their dreams were and what stood in the way of their reaching them. "One woman shared that she always wanted to be a secretary.... She said "I have six kids, and I don't have anyone to take care of them while I'm away." "Let's find out," I said. "Is there anybody in this group who would take care of six kids for a day or two a week while this woman gets some training here at the community college?"

The results were dramatic. Satir reports "Everyone found something.... The woman who took in the children became a licensed foster care person. In 12 weeks I had all these people off public welfare. I've not only done that once. I've done it many times." By accepting their need for mutual support, Satir demonstrated their ability to change the social context in which their problems occurred, and hence solve their problems. Her intervention with this one woman, for example, changed almost all the factors listed as correlating with depression in women (above). Satir explains about gender issues in particular, "I regard the emerging balance between women and men as being as earthshaking as the discovery that the world is round instead of flat." (Satir, 1988, p 379).

Note that Satir's aim was to demonstrate that people could be self-sufficient. However, for her, this self-sufficiency, this being "at cause" in their life, included their acting socially and asking for assistance from each other. She is encouraging interdependence rather than isolated independence.

Social Change Styles and Rapport

Once you have a clear social change goal, what actions enable you to achieve it? The answer depends partially on your own unique strengths and skills. Social change theorist Bill Moyer has proposed that "There are four different roles activists and social movements need to play in order to successfully create social change; *the citizen, rebel, change agent*, and *reformer*. Each role has different purposes styles, skills and needs, and can be played effectively or ineffectively.... Both individual activists and movement organisations need to understand that social movements require *all four* roles, and that participants and their organisations can choose which ones to play depending on their own makeup and the needs of the movement." (Moyer, 2001, p. 21).

Citizens frame the social change needed as a way to more fully express the true, underlying values that society has already committed itself to. They feel part of their society. They describe their activism as being a way to be a good citizen and support the true needs of their society. They urge society to move away from those things that don't really fit with its own highest ideals. For example, the African American activist Martin Luther King described his aim as to "fulfil the American dream, not to destroy it." (Quoted in Moyer, 2001, p. 11).

Rebels take action to get away from harmful social systems. They directly challenge society as it is. They describe their activism as a way to eliminate injustice and suffering. Often critical both of established society and utopian or reformist plans for a new society, they urge society first to confront and give up what is wrong. Rebuilding is for later. The Anarchist revolutionary Michael Bakunin stated a core Rebel value when he said "The urge to destroy is also a creative urge."

Change Agents organise and participate in community actions which are an alternative or a vocal opposition movement opposed to the established social systems. They urge society to create a new social order and see their movement as the kernel of this order. The creators of the original Soviets (workers councils) in Russia and the Collectives in the Spanish revolution were Change Agents.

Reformers work within mainstream systems to get the movement's aims expressed in concrete terms. They see social change as a process of convincing governments, community agencies and corporations to put new schemes into practice. They cooperate with existing agencies to build the new. New Zealand suffragette Kate Sheppard described her work in these terms.

On December 1st, 1955, African American Rosa Parks was arrested in Montgomery, Alabama, for refusing to give up her seat on the bus for a white person. For 381 days, the 50,000 strong black population of Montgomery boycotted the buses, until the United States supreme court overturned the Alabama segregation laws. Bill Moyer points out that in such a campaign all four of his MAP roles come into play. "The boycott effectively used all four MAP roles. The citizens kept the campaign grounded in the nation's widely held values of democracy and freedom, and their demands were based on the civil rights guaranteed by the U.S. Constitution. Many of the citizens were based in the Christian church, which was revered by the large majority of whites in Montgomery and within mainstream America. The rebels brought attention to the movement with the non-violent bus boycott campaign. The entire black community of Montgomery filled the social change agent role by its involvement in the boycott, mass meetings, and car-pooling. Finally, the reformers ultimately won the day through the court case, which was decided favourably by the U. S. Supreme Court." (Moyer, 2001, p. 120)

As Moyer notes, different personality styles lie behind the different social change roles. The study of how the brain works has led NLP developers to identify a number of key personality differences or "metaprograms" that commonly occur between people. Meta means above or beyond, and metaprograms are programs or strategies that operate above and beyond our everyday behaviours and strategies. There are over 50 such metaprograms (personality traits) tabulated in NLP (Bodenhamer and Hall, 1997). I believe two of these are of key significance when understanding the four social change roles. These two relevant metaprograms are:

- Sameness (Matching) vs Difference (Mismatching)
- Towards vs Away From

Here is a table summarising the relationship of these metaprograms to the social change roles.

Reformers match mainstream systems and move them towards new laws etc.	**Match**	**Citizens** match mainstream values, & move away from results not aligned with those.
Towards ←→ Away From		
Change Agents mismatch mainstream systems and move towards new systems.	**Mismatch**	**Rebels** mismatch mainstream systems and push society away from those systems.

Sameness and Difference

When people pay attention to the world, they can either notice mostly the similarities or mostly the differences (or some of each). People who notice sameness most (matchers) will also like things to stay the same, and they like to agree with others. Reformers and Citizens tend to use matching more. People who notice differences more (mismatchers) will also like to change, and they like to clarify differences with people. Change Agents and Rebels tend to use mismatching more. To the sameness person, a friend is someone who shares your views and does things together in the same way as you. To the differences person, a friend is someone who tells you "where they stand", opens your life up to new things, and respects your uniqueness. Using NLP questionnaires, we have found that most of the population identifies sameness and then notices the exceptions or differences within that (ie they are in the middle of the continuum).

Certain careers (the military, empathic counselling, factory process work, and nursing, for example) encourage paying attention to sameness. Other careers (such as accounting, legal work, quality control, university lecturing and political activism) encourage attention to differences. People who sort mostly for differences will feel interested when a project is described as "revolutionary", "new", "totally unique", "unheard of", and "a complete turn around". People sorting for sameness will prefer projects described as "maintaining", "identical in style", and "like earlier projects". People sorting for sameness and then noticing the exceptions to that will enjoy projects described as "better", "more advanced", "improved", "a further development"

To find out whether someone mainly pays attention to differences or to similarities in the context of their political work, you'd ask them, "What is the relationship between your work this year and your work last year?" In their home context, you could ask, "What is the relationship between the home you're living in now and the last home you lived in?" There are three main possible results of asking the question:

1) Sameness: It's exactly the same.
2) Sameness with exception: There's a lot of similarity except that it has developed.
3) Difference: It's totally different. OR What do you mean by "relationship?"

In a social change context, Citizens and Reformers are sameness focused. Rebels and Change Agents sort mainly for differences. How can you get these two different personality types to work together in a group? There are several things you can do to help others to get their pattern to work better for them, for example:

For working with sameness people:
- Build markers of familiarity into change processes for similarities people. Show them how to detect what will be the same or be preserved over the course of the changes.
- Give sameness people the task of monitoring ongoing processes needed for stability, and identifying what works already.

For working with differences people:
- Build differences and variations into any repetitive task for a differences person.
- Give differences people the task of identifying flaws, and thinking up new ideas.
- Give differences people something to disagree with that leaves the things you want stable.
- Invite differences people to consider a decision from the other side, using phrases such as: "Maybe you **don't** want to do it this new way?" "It's a good idea, **do you not think so?**"
- Do *not* use the words "have to" and "must" with differences people, unless you want them to disagree. Use "could".

The Advantage Of Mismatching

Much of social change depends on the ability to mismatch. As George Bernard Shaw said in his 1903 "Maxims for Revolutionists", "The reasonable man adapts himself to the world; the unreasonable one persists in trying to adapt the world to himself. Therefore, all progress depends on the unreasonable man." (Shaw, 1980). Eddie Yuen argues in a paragraph on "The Power Of Negative Thinking" in the globalisation movement that "It is important for the movement not to abandon the powerful stance of *refusal*.... The movement so far has helped to precipitate a crisis in the affirmative ideology of capitalist globalisation (e.g. the mantra that market democracy represents the "end of history") by maintaining a broadly "negative" position – "one no, many yeses."

The Advantage of Matching

There is an important effect of matching that people in social change groups benefit from understanding. Matching is the basis for keeping a group working together, because matching is what creates "rapport".

Rapport is the sense that you have a common bond with someone, that you're on the same wavelength, that you see eye-to-eye. It's the feeling of shared understanding that happens between old friends or lovers. If you want to have close friends, lasting intimacy, a loving family life, co-operative work relationships, and the ability to influence others positively ... then what you're seeking is rapport.

Despite the fact that many people have spent their whole life searching for it, rapport is *easy* to create. There's only one thing you need to do: make your messages similar in form to those of the person you're with. What this means is that rapport is a result of matching! When your messages "pace" or "match" theirs, they'll actually be more willing to accept your suggestions and follow your lead. There are a number of things you can match in a persons behaviour to increase the chances that you will create this feeling of rapport.

1. **Voice**. You can match the volume (loudness), speed, tone (high or low), and timbre (individual quality, like rough or soft) of the voice when speaking with someone. You can also listen carefully to the words the person uses, and use similar wording. If someone has a problem and they talk about how gloomy life is, I talk about their search for the light at the end of the tunnel. If they talk about how bogged down they've been, I explore how they can loosen things up and break free.
2. **Eye contact.** Ever seen two people talking and both staring at the same spot on the ground? They're in rapport. Using your eyes to gesture similarly to the person you're with will help you to access the same kind of inner experience they have. Use a similar level of eye contact to what they feel comfortable with. This varies culturally. In New Zealand Maori and Pacific cultures, for example, eye contact is used far less than in European cultures.
3. **Gestures and general body position**.
4. **Breathing**. Co-ordinating your breathing with someone else is a very deep way to establish rapport. And yet this too is something you've done many times. When two people sleep together in the same room, their breathing naturally co-ordinates. If you breath in time with someone and then gradually slow your breathing down, they will tend to slow down. Many parents have learned to put their children to sleep using this kind of rapport process. By lying down beside the child and gradually slowing their breathing, they slow down the child's breathing until sleep begins.

You're already an expert at rapport. That's how you learned to speak your first language: by matching *perfectly* the way your parents and care-givers spoke. You did it so well you've even copied their accent! Being aware of your ability means you can use rapport in exactly those situations you need it most. Whenever you find yourself in a difficult interpersonal situation, in a conflict or a tense interaction, ask yourself "How can I increase the level of rapport here?"

In one class I taught rapport to, there was a student who worked at an elderly persons home. That very night, an elderly man was admitted in a manic state. Manic means he was rushing frantically round, talking at high speed, unable to rest, and voicing some fairly weird and wonderful beliefs about himself. Unperturbed, the student breathed in time with him for about two minutes, and then gently slowed her breathing down ... and he slowed down. In a few minutes he was back in a normal state. Of course, this isn't a cure for his manic psychiatric condition; but it did make the evening a lot easier for him.

The Research On Rapport

Examination of films and videotapes of therapy sessions and other conversations by communication researchers (Ivey et alia, 1996, p 60; Condon 1982, p 53-76; Hatfield et alia 1994) now confirms the importance of these rapport skills, which are called in the research "interactional synchrony" or "movement complementarity". Without having been trained to do so, people naturally match another person's body language and words in successful conversations.

William Condon has meticulously studied videotapes of conversations, confirming these patterns. He found that in a successful conversation, movements such as a smile or a head nod are matched by the other person within 1/15 of a second. Within minutes of beginning the conversation, the volume, pitch and speech rate (number of sounds per minute) of the peoples voices match each other. At the same time, the people match the type and rate of their breathing. Even general body posture is adjusted over the conversation so that the people appear to match or mirror each other. Elaine Hatfield, John Cacioppo and Richard Rapson, in their book *Emotional Contagion*, show that matching another person's behaviour in these detailed ways results in the transfer of emotional states from one person to another. If I feel happy, and you match my breathing, voice, gestures and smiles, you will begin to feel the same emotional state. This is the source of the feeling of empathy.

In 1995 a remarkable area of neurons (nerve cells) was discovered by brain researchers working at the University of Palma in Italy (Rizzolatti et alia, 1996; Rizzolatti and Arbib, 1998). The cells, now called "mirror neurons", are found in the pre-motor cortex of the brains of monkeys and apes as well as humans. In humans they form part of the specific area called Broca's area, which is also involved in the creation of speech. Although the cells are related to motor activity (i.e. they are part of the system by which we make kinesthetic responses such as moving an arm), they seem to be activated by visual input. When a monkey observes another monkey (or even a human) making a facial expression or body movement, or vocalising, the mirror neurons light up. As they do, the monkey appears to involuntarily copy the same movement it has observed visually. This ability to copy a fellow creatures actions as they do them has obviously been very important in the development of primate social intelligence. It enables us to identify with the person we are observing and to experience the emotions of fellow humans empathically. When this area of the brain is damaged in a stroke, copying another's actions becomes almost impossible. The development of speech has clearly been a result of this copying skill.

What does this mean for us as communicators in social change organisations? Firstly, it means that we benefit from developing the skills of breathing in time with others, adjusting our voice tonality to match theirs, and adjusting our posture and gestures to match theirs. Secondly, it emphasises the importance, once the sense of rapport has been established with someone who is distressed, of having the flexibility to gradually shift back to a healthy and resourceful style of breathing, speaking and acting. The purpose of getting in rapport with others is often to then assist them to move towards new goals; a process called in NLP "pacing and leading". By revealing the nonverbal basis of rapport, NLP has been able to add considerably to the skills which we can use to convey empathy.

The developers of NLP noted that the chance of one person being able to help someone else to change their behaviour was increased by the helper checking in words to ensure they could understand the person's reality first. "When you join someone else's reality by pacing them, that gives you rapport and trust, and puts you in a position to utilise their reality in ways that change it." (Bandler and Grinder, 1979, p 81).

Research identifying the effectiveness of restating the words or the meaning behind the words that people have said (*verbal* pacing; reflective listening) first emerged in the 1950s. There has been 50 years of continuing evidence for this core helping skill (Garfield, 1994; Lambert and Bergin, 1994, p 181, Fiedler 1951). For example, one of the ways that people often create anxiety for themselves is to make scary internal visual images. If I talk with the anxious person who is imagining scary pictures in their head, and I discuss what they can *see* as they sit beside me, there is an increased chance that when I gradually shift my comments to talk more about

41

kinesthetic (body sensation) relaxation, the person will follow my lead into the new experience of relaxation (Yapko, 1981).

Rapport In Social Change

In 1993, a solution was reached in the conflict between Palestine and Israel. Secret meetings were held in Oslo, Norway, between a Palestinian team led by Abu Ala and an Israeli team led by Yair Hirschfeld. Terje Roed-Larsen headed a group of Norwegian facilitators, trained in conflict resolution skills. On September 13, 1993, the Israeli Prime Minister Yitzhak Rabin and the PLO leader Yasser Arafat, sworn enemies for over five decades, shook hands and signed the Oslo Accord. Hatred and mistrust had shifted to co-operation.

How did this shift occur? Roed-Larsen explains (in Watkins and Rosegrant, 2001, p 152-153) "What I wanted was a pre-negotiating phase, because I thought there had to be confidence established on an emotional basis.... I also decided to treat the Israelis and the Palestinians exactly the same way; they should have the same cars, the same hotel rooms, the same food.... In pre-negotiations, the parties have to gain confidence. It's like a love story." Knowing the importance of verbal rapport himself, Abu Ala made a point of using the exact language that Israeli Foreign Minister Shimon Peres had been using. Israeli negotiator Uri Savir said with astonishment that Abu Ala "was speaking Peres' language. Abu Ala had read Peres' books." Sadly, the rapport of the Oslo meetings was not shared by the general populace, and on November 3, 1995, Prime Minister Rabin was assassinated as part of an Israeli backlash. The situation slid back to open warfare. There are lessons here about the risks of secret negotiations, but there are also important lessons about the power of rapport.

Noam Chomsky suggests that social change agents in general would benefit from better rapport skills. Explaining the problems that the movement faces internally, he says, "In part the problem is just divisiveness – it's passionate commitment to a very narrow position, and extreme intolerance of anyone who doesn't see it exactly the way you do. So if you have a slightly different view from the person next door on, say, abortion rights, it's a war – you can't even talk to each other, it's not an issue that you can even discuss. There's a lot of that on the left, and it's been very self-destructive. It's made the progressive movements, the sort of "left" movements, kind of unwelcome – because people don't like it; they see it, and they don't like it." (Chomsky, 2002, p 237-238).

In NLP we say that wherever your communication meets resistance, this is an indication that you do not have sufficient rapport with the person who is "resisting". Chomsky applies this principle to decisions about what action to take as a social change agent. Explaining why he was opposed to peace activists attacking missiles at US bases, he says "I don't think there's any question of principle involved in whether you should smash a missile nose-cone or not, it's not like a contract between you and God or something. The question is, what are the effects? .... Like, if you smash up a missile nose-cone in some town where people are working at the missile plant and there's no other way they can make a living, and they haven't heard of any reason why we shouldn't have missiles, that doesn't educate anybody, it just gets them mad at you.... **I mean you have to start with where the world is**. Like you don't start by saying, "Okay, lets overthrow transnational corporations" – because right now it's just not within range. So you start by saying, "Look, here's where the world is, what can we begin to do?" Well, you can begin to do things which will get people to understand better what the real source of power is, and just how much they can achieve if they get involved in political activism." (Chomsky, 2002, p 187, 191, emphasis mine).

Towards And Away From

When people motivate themselves to act, they can either notice mostly what they are wanting to change or move *away from* (the problems) or mostly the things they want to create or move *towards* (the solutions) or some of each. People who move Towards their desired outcomes are energized and excited by their goals, and may at times seem to naively not notice the problems they may face. Reformers and Change Agents (using Moyer's model of social change roles) tend to be motivated Towards more. People who move Away From undesirable problems more will be energized by challenges, and may at times seem to get "stuck" complaining about the various crises, challenges and unacceptable events they want to draw attention to. Citizens and Rebels tend to be motivated Away From more.

To the Towards person, what matters is the vision, the result that we are moving towards. They can explain in detail what results they want, but may be unclear about what the current situation is. To the Away From person, what matters is the challenge in the current situation. They can explain in detail what must be changed and why, but may be unclear exactly what they want instead. Using NLP questionnaires, we have found that about 40% of the population mainly uses Away From motivation, about 40% mainly uses Towards motivation, and about 20% uses both equally.

Certain career paths (medicine, insurance, and policing, for example) encourage paying attention to what is wrong and moving away from it.

Other career paths (such as tourism, artistic design and) encourage attention to desired results and moving towards these. People who are motivated Towards will feel interested when a project is described with words such as "achieving", "benefits", "advantages" and "what you've wanted". People who are motivated Away From will prefer projects described with words such as "solve", "avoid", "get rid of", "prevent", and "find out what's wrong".

To find out whether someone mainly motivates themselves Towards or Away From in the context of their political activism, you'd ask them, "Why is this work important to you?" In their home context, you could ask, "Why are you living where you live now?" There are three main possible results of asking the question:

4) Towards: Because it gets me what I want.
5) Away From: Because it helps me avoid what I don't want.
6) Towards and Away From: Because it get me what I want and avoids what I don't want.

On the day Nelson Mandela became president of South Africa, he revealed his ability to use both towards and away from language, saying "My government's commitment to create a people-centered society of liberty binds us to the pursuit of the goals... [Towards language] ... of freedom from hunger, freedom from deprivation, freedom from ignorance, freedom from suppression and freedom from fear. [Away From language]" (Quoted in Charvet, 1997, p 39)

Activists with different styles often debate over this difference in motivation style. In the globalisation movement, for example, Liza Featherstone, Doug Henwood and Christian Parenti say "The movement is also undergoing a fascinating rhetorical shift, as activists reject terms like "antiglobalization", which emphasised – not very lucidly – what they're against, in favour of slogans like "Another World Is Possible" which dare to evoke the possibility of radically different economic arrangements. What would that other world look like? Activists must engage that question." (Featherstone et alia, 2004, p. 314). Note that even their "frame" for this change is Towards – the change in attitude is a "fascinating rhetorical shift" to things that activists are "in favour of". On the other hand, Eddie Yuen warns "In short, the movement should acknowledge the tremendous rhetorical power that accompanies as stance of negation and refusal, and not feel pressured into excessively diverting its energies towards hammering out blueprints which are unrealistic at best and divisive at worst." (Yuen, 2004, p. xxii). Once again, even Eddie Yuen's reasons for using Away From motivation are described mainly in Away From terms, avoiding things that are "unrealistic at best and divisive at worst".

How can you get these two different personality types to work together in a group? There are several things you can do to help others to get their pattern to work better for them, for example:

For working with Towards people:
- Show them how checking for possible ecology issues will help in reaching goals more effectively.
- Give them the task of identifying and designing the progress towards goals.

For working with Away From people:
- Explain the problems that setting a clear goal will help solve.
- Describe goal-setting as creating deadlines for solving the problems.
- Give them the task of identifying, monitoring and solving the problems in a plan.
- Have them do something (anything) and then "fix it" as a way of reaching the outcome you are aiming for.

The Polish Solidarity Movement

We can see the four different change styles at work in the monumental changes that shook Poland as a society in the 1970s and 1980s. In the midst of these changes, it was easy for people to think that there was one correct way to achieve change. We can now see that all four change styles worked together to shift Polish society into the twenty first century. Here I briefly give an example or two from each role.

Jerzy Popiełuszko (citizen)
Blessed Father Jerzy Popiełuszko (1947-1984) was a Roman Catholic priest who argued that the Socialist regime needed to be changed because it did not fit with the deeper Christian values that Polish society had been founded on. In his preaching he explained moral aspects of the painful reality of everyday life, in the light of the teachings of the Church. He did not try to change the Church to which he belonged, but simply to apply its message more congruently in the rest of society. He was thus able to say the unthinkable: that the "unchristian" aspects of Polish socialism needed to change. His voice was one of the first raised against the old regime, and he was one of the first to be silenced in his murder in 1984.

Lech Wałęsa, Anna Walentynowicz (rebels)
Lech Wałęsa (1943-) was an electrician and organiser of the Solidarity movement, famous for his charismatic and challenging style. The organiser

of several strikes in the 1970s, he was continually laid off for his activism and was jobless for long periods. Accepting the Nobel Peace prize, he later said "When I recall my own path of life I cannot but speak of the violence, hatred and lies." This contrasts dramatically with Popiełuszko's patient approach. When the community needed this rebellious approach, he was a hero, but Wałęsa was later criticized for his confrontational style and for instigating "war at the top," whereby former Solidarity allies clashed with one another, causing annual changes of government. He agreed to stand for government only because he felt that he "had to". Anna Walentynowicz (1929-2010) was a welder and crane operator. Her firing in August 1980 was the event that ignited the strike at the Lenin Shipyard in Gdańsk that very quickly paralyzed the Baltic coast and a began giant wave of strikes in Poland. The Interfactory Strike Committee [MKS] based in the Gdańsk shipyard eventually transformed itself into Solidarity trade union. Early Solidarity pamphlets described her as a "thorn in the side" of the government, and she became known as the iron woman for her strength of opposition. Like many rebels, Wałęsa and Walentynowicz were the driving force of change, but found themselves dissatisfied with the results of their work. They continued to rebel against the new regime too.

Jacek Kuroń (change agent)
Jacek Kuroń (1934-2004) was a youth worker who gradually shifted from being a staunch defender of Marxism to being a left wing opponent. During the strikes of July and August 1980, Kuroń organized an information network for workers across the country, seeing this as the kernel of a future workers democracy. He launched his famous slogan, "Don't burn the committees [meaning the local party buildings], set up your own" in order to encourage workers to see Solidarity as a positive force rather than merely a rebellion. He organised groups to run their own communities as alternative societies, growing vegetables and self-managing their apartments etc. In 2000, after the changes in Poland, Kuroń and his wife Danuta founded the Jan Józef Lipski Common University in Teremiski. He subsequently became the first dean of this alternative university, continuing his change agent role rather than joining the new system or continuing to rebel.

Tadeusz Mazowiecki (reformer)
Tadeusz Mazowiecki (1927-) was a magazine editor who held government office under the old regime 1961-1972 and then ended up being Poland's first non-communist Prime Minister in 1989. Mazowiecki's government managed to carry out many fundamental reforms in a short period. The political system was thoroughly changed; a full range of civil freedoms as well as a multi-party system were introduced and the country's emblem and name were changed (from the People's Republic of Poland to the Republic

of Poland). On December 29, 1989, fundamental changes in the Polish Constitution were made. In 1989, in his first parliamentary speech in Sejm, Mazowiecki talked about a "thick line" (*gruba linia*): "We draw a thick line on what has happened in the past. We will answer for only what we have done to help Poland to rescue her from this crisis from now on". Originally, as Mazowiecki explains, the phrase meant non-liability of his government for damages done to the national economy by previous governments. Media led by Adam Michnik's left-leaning Gazeta Wyborcza later rephrased the term as a "thick stroke" (*gruba kreska*), essentially crossing out the communist past and going easy on the misdoings of the communists. Mazowiecki was the quintessential reformer, fitting a system back together after the change, codifying the changes, and signalling that the time of major change was now over.

Without all these four roles being filled, Poland could not have transitioned out of the domination of the Soviet Union. Of course, the Polish state has had problems since these times, but history is never finished. The breakthrough was enough to radically change the lives of people, not just in Poland, but in many other places in Eastern Europe.

Notice that as a generalization, the four roles come into prominence in a sequence, which I call "The wheel of change". Using terminology that makes sense also in personal change experiences, the four steps on the wheel are Auditor (i.e. the role of checking what doesn't fit with our current shared values. Auditor = Citizen), Rebel (i.e. the role of pointing out that the system needs to change to respect the challenges we have discovered), Innovator (i.e. the role of demonstrating with specific real life examples that a solution is possible Innovator = Change Agent) and Reformer (i.e. the role of reorganising the system so that it incorporates the new learnings from this process.)

Reframing

Challenging Assumed Meanings

NLP offers a number of models for understanding how social activism succeeds in altering the course of history. One is reframing. Reframing is based on the awareness that events in themselves don't have one specific meaning. Human beings give them meanings. The NLP term for such "meanings" is "frames". David Snow and Robert Benford are social movement theorists who proposed that *all* social action is in fact re-framing. They say that activists "...are actively engaged in the production of meaning for participants, antagonists, and observers.... They frame or assign meaning to and interpret relevant events and conditions in ways that are intended to mobilize potential adherents and constituents, to garner bystander support, and to demobilize antagonists." (Snow and Benford, 1988, p 197). As an example, they studied Martin Luther King's framing of African American issues as based on Christian and traditional American democratic values.

There are two steps to this reframing process. The first step is to be able to "deframe", or to challenge the frame through which someone is viewing events. "Deframing" is done in NLP with a series of questions based on the work of Noam Chomsky.

We get a sense of how Noam Chomsky himself applies this ability to deframe, from his method of discussion in public forums. He is a skilled user of what NLP would call *metamodel* questioning. Since he developed the model behind the *metamodel* (Transformational Grammar; see Chomsky, 1957), this is hardly surprising. Metamodel questions are designed to get a person to shift back from the "surface structure" of their own theories and "frames" for viewing reality, to the underlying sensory experiences that the person built these surface structures from (to use Chomsky's original terms). They are designed to challenge the frames through which the person is viewing reality. Reframing, which we'll look at next, is a way of offering new and more useful frames.

The point of learning the meta-model, however, is not to rush out and ask people all these challenging questions. The meta-model questions are "challenging" responses. They need to be used in a context of rapport building and reflective listening (as described in the previous section on matching and rapport). The most important way to use this list of questions for now is to pay *attention* to your own and others' use of the patterns. Once you can hear these patterns (and there are metamodel patterns in every sentence, including this one) you have valuable clues about what "frames" people are using to view their experience of the world through.

The following exchange shows how Chomsky uses metamodel questions himself:

"Man: Dr. Chomsky, I just want to ask a question on this topic: Daniel Ortega [Nicaraguan President, Sandinista Party] was in power for how long, a decade?
Yes
Man: And yet he lost the election.
Why "And yet"?
Man: Well, he had control of that country for ten years.
What does that mean, "He had control of it"?
Man: He controlled the press.
He did not. In fact, Nicaragua is the only country I know of in history that allowed a major opposition press [La Prensa] to operate while it was being attacked – a press which was calling for the overthrow of the government by violence...." (Chomsky, 2002, p 109)

Here Chomsky challenges two metamodel patterns: the presuppositional phrase "and yet", and the unspecified verb "had control of". By challenging these patterns, he has the person go back to the original sensory experiences from which they built their current "frame". This sensory-specific statement can then be shown to be false using historical data. Asking questions such as "Why *and yet*?" or "What does that mean specifically?" enables Chomsky to create an entirely different frame on current events compared to observers who accept the frames presented in the media.

Following is a listing of the key metamodel patterns to listen for, and the questions to challenge them. To use these metamodel questions effectively, it's important to use reflective listening first, to restate or acknowledge what the person said, and then to gently inquire.

1. **Mind Read:** Sometimes a person's way of explaining events contains beliefs that are 'supernatural', such as **mind reading**, (for example: 'I know what he thinks of me). The metamodel suggests you ask how this process is happening: 'How, specifically, do you know? What do you see or hear?'

2. **Value Judgement with Lost Performative:** When a person says something is "wrong" or "right", "good" or "bad", they often don't say who is **performing** this **value judgement**. You could ask: "According to whom?" For example: "It's wrong to accept charity." "According to whom?

Who believes it's wrong?" This question helps the person identify whose world-view they are using: is it their own? Is it their parent's? Is it some political theorist whose work they admire? Who is the "lost performer" of the value judgment? Whatever the answer, the question reminds them that it's only an opinion.

3. **Cause-Effect:** Another "supernatural" belief is that one person can make an emotional response happen inside another person's body - that one person can **cause effects** in another body without touching them. For example: "You make me feel very powerless." A metamodel response might be: "How, specifically, does what I do cause you to feel powerless."

4. **Complex Equivalent:** Sometimes a person claims that an event has a meaning way beyond what it needs to mean. For example: "He never comes to our meetings so he obviously doesn't give a damn what happens", or "If we argue it means the group isn't working". These claims suggest that "giving a damn" is an **equivalent** of "coming to meetings", or that "arguing" is an equivalent of "a group not working". A metamodel response to challenge this "equivalence" is: "How does ... mean ... ?" for example: "How does an argument mean that the group "sn't working?"

5. **Universal Quantifier:** If a person claims that something "always" happens, "never" happens, happens with "everyone" or with "no-one", the metamodel suggests you ask about this **universal quantity**, by repeating the same word, for example: "Always?", "No one?".

6. **Modal Operator of Impossibility:** Sometimes a person talks in a **"mode of impossibility"**: they believe that certain things are "impossible" for them. If a person says "I can't..." , the metamodel response could be either: "What stops you?" or "What would happen if you did?" For example: "I can't tell my husband what I really think of his sexist jokes". "What would happen if you did?"

7. **Modal Operator of Necessity:** At other times a person talks from the **"mode of necessity"** (of "have to" or "must"). If a person says "I must..." or "I have to...", the metamodel response would be: "What would happen if you didn't?" In both modes of impossibility and modes of necessity, the person's world-view assumes that things have to be the way they are. Your question challenges that limit.

8. **Unspecified Verb:** A person may also describe what happens in such general terms that you don't know who did what to whom. The **verbs** (action words) in their sentences are **unspecified**. You could, then, ask for this information, for example:

• "My brother annoys me all the time." "How, specifically, does he annoy you?"
• "You've hurt me very much." "How, specifically, have I hurt you?"
• "People are always picking on me." "Which people are picking on you, and how, specifically, do they pick on you?"

9. **Deletion:** Sometimes a person simply misses out important parts of a sentence, leaving you to guess what they have **deleted**. The metamodel suggests you actually ask what these deleted things are. For example:
• "I can't cope with this." "What, specifically, can't you cope with?"
• "The things I do really confuse me." "What things do you do?"
• "I'm sad." "What are you sad about?" Such questions help the person explain what is wrong in a sensory specific way.

10) **Presupposition:** Often the person's sentence simply assumes the existence of "things" or assumes the possibility of actions. In order to "understand" the sentence, you'd need to accept the presuppositions. As an example, here is a statement from Adolf Hitler's Mein Kampf (Hitler, 1943, p 655). "Our task, the mission of the National Socialist movement, is to bring our own people to such political insight that they will not see their goal for the future in the breath-taking sensation of a new Alexander's conquest, but in the industrious work of the German plow, to which the sword need only give soil. It goes without saying that the Jews announce the sharpest resistance to such a policy. Better than anyone else they sense the significance of this action for their own future."

This statement, first written in 1925, Hitler reveals here the kind of presuppositional thinking that led to the holocaust. He is so sure of his mind-reading that he says "It goes without saying…" (ie it is presupposed). This kind of **presupposition** is one of the main dangers in Hitler's speeches and writing. He was convinced that he was living in a world where all Jews hated him and "his people". This presupposition did not even need proving to him. The simple metamodel response would be to ask "How do you know…" For example, "How do you know that the Jews announce the sharpest resistance to such a policy." For fun, you might like to practice using the other metamodel questions (above) to unpack the rest of this historically disturbing paragraph.

Meaning Reframe

Once you can identify and challenge frames in someone's statement, you can also construct more useful frames. The aim is not to be able to talk without using any presuppositions etc. It is to consciously choose those presuppositions that are functional and useful in the real world. Let me give an example. Dame Whina Cooper is remembered as the foundation president of the New Zealand Maori Women's Welfare League and leader of the 1975 Maori Land protest march (King, 1991). Her respect in the Maori community was not earned easily however. Soon after her election by the Welfare League she was speaking at a hui [gathering] in Taupo when a woman stood up and criticised her. Who was Cooper, the woman asked, to come high-handedly around the country telling them what to do? The meeting was tense, as people waited for her reply. A welfare officer offered to field the complaint but Cooper said she would deal with it.

Whina Cooper announced "I am so pleased to hear somebody talk like that, because when I hear something like that I know our Maori women will always be strong, will always be leaders. I'm so glad this person here feels big enough to tell me off. Yes, e hoa [friend], you're right. I'm nothing. I come from a nikau house with a dirt floor. I've got no education. All the other women you've mentioned, Te Puea and the others, they're all much more important than me. They're the ones. But remember this, e hoa. I didn't want to come here. I didn't want this job. But I was picked by the Maori women of New Zealand to come to you, to knit the people together. And I'm only trying to do that job because they asked me to." The meeting swung behind Cooper right away. Intuitively, she had begun her response by acknowledging the speaker and then "reframing" their criticism. Let me explain what I mean by "reframing". Many people at the meeting were tense after a woman's criticism. They thought that "disagreement means things are going badly." Whina Cooper said in effect, "disagreement doesn't mean things are going wrong. It means people are strong enough to speak up, and that means things are right!" She *reframed* or refiltered the experience, offering a new meaning.

The question Whina Cooper had asked herself was "What else could this situation mean, that would be *useful*?" It's a question that all highly successful communicators ask themselves. Oprah Winfrey is one of the world's most successful television presenters. Yet when she was a child she was the victim of horrific sexual abuse. Lots of people told her that *meant* that her life was damaged. Oprah decided it could have another meaning: it *could mean* that she was able to speak out and help people around the world who have lived in fear. Her talk-back TV show achieves exactly that.

That's the power of meaning reframing. To restate, events in themselves don't have one specific meaning. Human beings give them meanings. When someone tells you that their husband died last week; you don't know what that "means". You only know what the sensory specific event was. The meaning depends on how they filter that event. They may feel happy that they are free of an oppressive relationship, or glad that their husband is free of pain, or grief stricken that he is gone, or guilty that they didn't do more for him. Meaning is a result of our filtering processes, and a meaning reframe offers new filters.

In offering a meaning reframe, it will often help to reflective listen (to pace the person's own frame) first; to say "So you thought that the event meant…. I think it could mean…." When the person feels that you have understood their meaning, they are more willing to listen to yours. Oprah Winfrey might say "So you thought my unhappy childhood meant I would be damaged for life. I think it means I'm in an ideal situation to speak out on behalf of other children and get some changes." Kate Sheppard might have said "So you thought our losing the vote meant we were failing. I think our temporary defeat means that many others will now be drawn to our cause."

Context Reframing

A related question to "What else could this mean that's useful?" is "*Where or when else* would this be useful?" Award winning New Zealand writer Janet Frame, admitted to a psychiatric hospital as schizophrenic, was considered too withdrawn and too "involved in her own mental fantasy", by her doctors. These were the very skills that later, in the context of her writing career enabled her to win literary prizes internationally. Just in time, her doctor (Dr Blake Palmer) discovered that Frame had won a literary prize for her first book "The Lagoon". Frame was listed for a leucotomy (brain surgery), but after reading of the prize Dr Palmer announced "I've decided you should stay as you are. I don't want you changed". For that moment he had stepped out of his medical world view and asked "Where or when else would this behaviour be useful?"

In 1975, Greg Newbold was sent to Paremoremo prison to begin serving a seven and a half year sentence for a drug offence. Most people in his situation find their daily life too limited to be of much use. By 1978, Newbold had presented his Masters thesis on the social organisation of prisons. By 1982 he had published a book on his prison life ("The Big Huey"). 1987 saw him Doctor Greg Newbold, of the Sociology Department at Canterbury University. He had found one remarkable answer to the question "Where or when else would this be *useful*?"

Many brilliant inventions are context reframes. On a September morning in 1928, Scottish scientist Alexander Fleming was checking a culture plate he was using in his study of bacteria. The culture plate was spoiled: a mould was growing in the corner. Fleming was about to throw the plate out, and was complaining to his friend D.M. Price about the nuisance, when he noticed something odd.

"That's funny", he muttered, and took the plate off to study it. Everywhere near the mould, the bacteria had died. Although Fleming showed this phenomenon to many other scientists that day, none were interested. Only Fleming had made the context reframe. The penicillium mould, a nuisance in the culture plate, would be a lifesaver if you could apply it to infections on human beings. Fleming had discovered Penicillin, the first antibiotic. He did it with that key question: "Where or when else would this be useful?"

Again, in using this skill with another person, it is important to pace their reality first. Imagine being a counsellor working with Greg Newbold when he was first put in prison in 1975. To say "Cheer up; this will be really useful if you ever want to write a book about prisons." would be rather challenging, and unlikely to succeed. It would help to reflect first. "So this has been a pretty awful time for you, and it seems like your daily life is going to be too limited to do anything useful over the next years. I think some of the experiences you have here could be really useful if you were ever in the situation of studying social policy."

Noam Chomsky: Social Comment As Reframing

Let's take an example of this reframing in social change work. Much of what Noam Chomsky does as a speaker is to reframe events so that they have more useful meanings. Talking about the sense of hopelessness that those involved in social change sometimes have, he notes "Take the so-called "Gulf War" – it wasn't really a war, it was a slaughter, but take the Gulf Slaughter. It led to tremendous depression on the left, because people felt like they weren't able to do anything about it. Well, if you just think about it for a minute, you realize that it was exactly the opposite; it was probably the greatest victory the peace movement has ever had. The Gulf War was the first time in history that there were huge demonstrations and protests *before* a war started – that's never happened before. In the case of the Vietnam war, it was five years before anybody got out in the streets; this time, there were massive demonstrations with hundreds of thousands of people involved *before* the bombing even started." (Chomsky, 2002, p 328).

The idea of reframing is that events in themselves do not have "meanings". We add meanings to them. Sometimes we add meanings simply by the way we label them; as in the case of the Gulf "War" of 1991. In that war there were 35,000 civilian Iraqi deaths, and over 6,000 retreating Iraqi soldiers were buried alive by US tanks with ploughs mounted in front, while the coalition forces suffered zero fatalities (Wright, 2003). Chomsky redefines these events as a "slaughter" rather than a "war". He then redefines the actions of the peace movement, organizing hundreds of thousands of demonstrators before the war began, as a success rather than a failure, and points out that this reframe could have saved people on the left from a lot of depression.

Given his passion for reframing, it is no wonder that Chomsky can even see a global sense of hopelessness as something positive. He argues: "I really don't think there's been a better period in modern history for organizing towards that than there is right now actually.... So what we're faced with is a combination of a very high degree of disillusionment, and a very low degree of hope and perception of alternatives. And that's exactly where serious organizers ought to be able to step in." (Chomsky, 2002, p 362). This is an interesting comment in terms of Political Process Opportunities theory, developed by Sydney Tarrow and others. Tarrow's claim was that social movements emerge when there are new political contexts which provide opportunities. Tarrow says of such opportunities "...while they do not on their own "explain" social movements, they play the strongest role in triggering general episodes of contention." (Tarrow, 1998, p 199). Chomsky's comment suggests that such "opportunities" are themselves the result of reframing.

Richard Bolstad

Anchoring

At the turn of the Century, a Russian scientist named Ivan Pavlov (1849-1936) was studying digestion in dogs. He noticed that the dogs began salivating <u>before</u> they were given meat - as soon as they saw their feeder or even as soon as they heard the person's footsteps. Pavlov found that if he sounded a tuning fork immediately before feeding the dogs each time, after a few meals he could simply sound the turning fork and the dogs would salivate. The dogs would salivate even though there was no meat available, because salivating was "anchored" in their minds to the experience of hearing the tuning fork (Pavlov, 1927).

The dogs didn't *plan* to salivate. This unconscious response was associated, or *anchored*, in an equally unconscious way to the sound of the turning fork. All of us have had similar experiences. Hearing a song, on the radio, that you haven't heard for many years can <u>anchor</u> you back to the memories of that time when you heard it years ago. You begin to *feel* the feelings you had back then. The whole state you were in at the time is recreated by the anchor of that music. All the strategies used at that time are reactivated by the anchor (for example, perhaps the ability to perform a dance you haven't done since hearing that music last time. Anchoring can happen in any sense. A specific sound (auditory), sight (visual), taste (gustatory), smell (olfactory), or touch (kinesthetic) can anchor the entire state originally associated with it.

Let's be clear that anchoring is not an invention of Pavlov's. In fact, anchoring is a continuously occurring part of life. By developing techniques based on anchoring we are not adding anything new to the world; we are giving people control over what is already happening. State and corporate marketing agencies already use this process, when they place the national flag behind the leader's desk, play the national anthem or some song that was popular when you were young, or when they show people partying and having fun combined with an image of their carbonated beverage. These processes deliberately re-create states of mind that the marketers want you to experience (such as patriotism, thirst and excitement). What anchoring shows you is how to reclaim and use this same phenomenon in your brain to motivate you to get things done, to relax you so you can make clear decisions or work easily in a group... and to re-inspire yourself with your life mission on a daily basis.

The process of anchoring was "rediscovered" by NLP co-developers Richard Bandler and John Grinder (1979, p 79-136). It can be used to take any emotional state that a person has experienced at some time in their life,

56

and "connect" it to situations they would like to experience that state in. In a controlled research study published in Germany (Reckert, 1994), Horst Reckert describes how in one session he was able to remove students' test anxiety using this simple technique, described below. In another study, John Craldell discusses the use of anchoring to access a "self-caring-state" useful for adult children of alcoholics (Craldell, 1989), and in a third study, Mary Thalgott discusses the use of anchors to support children with learning disabilities (Thalgott, 1986). For an anchor to work, four things have to happen.

1) State: When the anchor (say the tuning fork) first occurs, the person must be in the state you'd like to be able to reproduce later. If Pavlov first rang the turning fork in a situation where the dogs weren't very hungry, it wouldn't be associated with a strong enough state. When he rang it later, hoping to re-anchor salivation, the effect wouldn't be so strong then either. He needed to use the anchor when the dogs were REALLY hungry.
2) Precise Timing: Similarly, Pavlov had to first ring the turning fork exactly when the dogs salivated, not five minutes before or after.
3) Uniqueness: The anchor has to be unique. If Pavlov's dogs heard turning forks at other times during the day, he'd need to find a more unique sound to use as an anchor.
4) Repeatable: If you want to use an anchor later, you have to be able to repeat it. Imagine that Pavlov had a huge gong which he sounded. It's very unique, but when he wanted to show off the dogs' new trick at the Russian Academy of Sciences, he'd have to carry in the gong as well.

Because anchoring is always happening, and is not a conscious process, most people have picked up a few anchors they could do without. In my work as a counsellor I've assisted many people to change such experiences using an NLP process called collapsing anchors. Here's one example.

John asked if I could assist him to be in a better state presenting his ideas to a group. He said he got incredibly anxious about standing up in front of a group: it was associated with a lot of bad memories - times he'd felt humiliated as a kid. It puzzled him, because he knew that there were some smaller groups where he could feel completely at ease. He knew he had important things to say in the large groups he was working with, but something about it "triggered him off." For John, talking to groups of more than ten people - even just being in a larger group - *anchored* him into a state where he felt nervous.   All his resources, his confidence and intelligence, weren't available once he saw people's faces looking at him.

I explained to John that I'd use anchoring by pressing on the back of his knuckles, to solve this problem. One knuckle would become an anchor for "being in front of a large group" and another knuckle would be an anchor for confidence and relaxation. Once I'd set up these two anchors, by pressing them both at once I would cause the two states to reconnect in his brain. In that way the resources of confidence and relaxation would be *automatically and unconsciously* associated with the group situation. John was sceptical but ready to try anything.

I started off by anchoring resources. I asked John to remember a time had felt <u>really</u> relaxed, maybe on holiday. I had him step into his body at that time and what it felt like, see what he saw, listen to the sounds there, and listen to anything he might say to himself. I watched him carefully as he re-experienced this time. As he got back into the <u>state</u> of relaxation fully (rather than just "thinking" about it) there were changes in his voice, posture, breathing, skin tone and so on.

I needed to see and hear these changes to know that John was fully in the <u>state</u> I wanted. As he remembered especially the things he saw, I pressed one of his knuckles. As he remembered the things he heard, I pressed it again. As he remembered the feeling in his body, I pressed once more. He didn't have any internal self-talk at the time. I had now anchored a relaxed state with a unique pressure on his knuckle. I asked him to stand up and stretch, to "clear the screen". Next I went through the same procedure with a time John had felt incredibly confident. Again I watched for the non-verbal shifts that told me he was in a confident state before anchoring on the <u>same</u> knuckle. I had now "stacked" this knuckle "anchor" with two resourceful states.

After clearing the screen again, I asked John to remember being in front of a group he'd been working with recently. His whole body immediately tensed up and his voice got shaky. I anchored this state on a <u>different</u> knuckle, and told him to clear the screen. Now one knuckle was linked to his resources, and one to the problem situation. I simply pressed down on both knuckles at once and waited for the change. John's eyes flickered and I began to see his body relax. I held the resource anchor down a few seconds longer.

Then I asked John "Now, try and think of that group."

John frowned. "It's funny" he said, "I'm finding it hard to even remember what it looked like. But it feels totally different."

"Try and get back the feeling you used to have," I suggested.

"No, I can't do it," he said after a pause.

"You used to be good at that." I reminded him.

"That's right, but now it just feels relaxed."

I asked John to think ahead to his next group meeting, and asked what happened when he thought of that. "Well," he smiled, "I can imagine it being okay: But I don't know. I'll tell you on Monday."

However, he saw me the next day with some dramatic news. "Last night," he bubbled over, "I went to plan what I would say at the meeting. And I thought, "This'll be a drag, because I've always found psyching myself up for that is pretty challenging. But somehow it was completely easy. In fact I enjoyed it so much I worked out a whole new proposal that I wanted to sound out with them."

I nodded. "So I guess now you're convinced that Friday's meeting will go okay."

"Well, I'll wait and see."

Not a man who's easily convinced. The Monday after the meeting he was finally willing to accept it. He announced with pride, "For the first time in my life, I felt totally relaxed talking to thirty people."

To me as the person who assisted John, what's most exciting is that John overcame his "problem" with his own resources. His brain already knew how to be relaxed and confident . It just needed the neurological connection from this state to the group situation. Even though collapsing anchors is one of the simplest NLP techniques, my colleagues and I have at times successfully used it with phobias, obsessional disorders, learning disorders, insomnia, depression and many other situations where a person's resources need reconnecting to new areas of their life. However, I'd also want to add that usually, there are other processes I'd expect to be using in those situations, as well as anchoring.

Aligning Neurological Levels

A more sophisticated process for using anchoring is to anchor your sense of inspiration about the social change that you are wanting to achieve and link it to the specific situations that you have found a challenge. NLP Trainer Robert Dilts calls this "Aligning neurological levels".

Different perspectives change the meaning of an event (reframe it). NLP trainer Robert Dilts points out that you could respond to a crisis at a number of different "neurological levels", from narrow focus to big picture.

1) **Environment:** The simplest way to create change is to change the environment or move to another environment.
2) **Behaviour:** Change can be created at this level by showing the person exact steps to take.
3) **Capabilities:** Deeper change can be achieved by learning whole new skills
4) **Beliefs and Values:** Fundamental changes involves changing beliefs about what is possible and what is worth doing.
5) **Identity:** Even deeper change can occur by getting a new experience of who I am as a person and what I am doing in my life.
6) **Spirituality:** The deepest changes come from a new sense of connection to everything that is, to history, to the universe, to life, to God, to consciousness etc.

To experience this practically,

1. Choose a problem you've had, and would like to change in a fundamental way.

2. Stand somewhere with plenty of space in front of you (enough to step forward six times). Think of the environment where the problem (that you want to move away from) occurs. Notice what you see, and listen to the sounds there.

3. Take a step forward. Consider what you actually do and say in the problem situation. Just run a movie of what happens with that problem.

4. Take another step forward. When you do those things, what capabilities, what skills are you using (perhaps habits that you wish you didn't use, but that happen automatically, or skills that don't seem to work for you)? And what skills are you not using?

5. Take another step forward. Consider what beliefs you are acting on in that situation. What do you find yourself believing about your potential or lack of it, and about the situation that you want to change? Also notice what feels important to you when you are in that situation (it may be just changing the situation)?

6. Take another step forward. Who are "you" in this situation? What kind of person are you in this situation? If we only knew you in this situation, what kind of person would we experience you as?

7. Take another step forward, and remember that you are here for a reason. You only got yourself into that situation because, in a wider sense, you're trying to create a better world. Perhaps you were trying to do something else as part of this purpose, and this happened unexpectedly. Or perhaps you planned to be in this situation, and then discovered how challenging it is. You may not know in words clearly what that reason is, but notice it exists now.

8) Realise that this "reason" connects you to something vast. You may think of it as the story of humanity, as God, as the universe and the laws of nature, as consciousness or beingness, or just as humanity. But imagine it as a vast source of energy, in front of you now. Take another step forward, into that source of energy. Feel its power, its vastness.

9. As you feel that power, take a step back and notice how that power gives renewed strength to your mission in this situation, your reason for acting. Take another step back and feel how that power transforms your sense of who you are. Take another step back and feel how that power changes what you believe about that situation you were considering; changes what seems important there. Take another step back and notice how it changes what skills you can use there, gives you new choices. Take another step back and be aware of how using those skills, with that vast power, changes what you will do and say there. Take another step back and be aware how those actions, done with that power, will change the situation itself.

10. Thank that power.

Resilience, Recovery and Chronicity

As I guide people through these processes, some people discover that their own thinking style gets in the way of them being able to anchor positive states. The study of traumatic events such as war and tsunami offers another frame for thinking about these unhelpful thinking styles.

When a traumatic event occurs, a neural network is set up in the brain with memories of the event, instructions about attempted responses, a time/place coding (Hippocampus) and an emergency rating (Amygdala). If the emergency rating is low enough, a pattern of **Resilience** occurs, where the person is distressed by the event but able to keep functioning normally. If the rating is high enough then at least for some time a PTSD-style response will occur and the person will have severe difficulty performing normal daily functions. The neurotransmitters which connect the new neural network are those present at the time, which is likely to include a lot of transmitters such as noradrenalin and adrenaline. The aim of the Amygdala connection is so that in any future similar events, the neural network will have override priority and be able to stop the Frontal Cortex (Conscious Goalsetting etc) from endangering life by thinking through a planned response.

While this mostly saves lives, occasionally it results in a panic response which is triggered accidentally by sensory stimuli that are themselves not dangerous. In that case most people will gradually edit the neural network over the next couple of months so that it no longer interferes with everyday functioning, a pattern called **Recovery**. Some people have a pre-existing thinking style which makes recovery difficult (e.g. a pattern of constantly checking in case something bad is about to happen again) and they will then continue to have problems long term, a pattern called **Chronicity**. Which of the 3 patterns will occur is determined by the pre-existing thinking style and model of the world, previous experience of similar trauma, the severity of the current traumatic events, and the social support available at the time of the current trauma.

The American Psychological Association says research suggests that research supports several "Ways to Build Resilience", in order to cope with traumatic events.

- to maintain good relationships with close family members, friends and others;
- to avoid seeing crises or stressful events as unbearable problems;
- to accept circumstances that cannot be changed;
- to develop realistic goals and move towards them;
- to take decisive actions in adverse situations;
- to look for opportunities of self-discovery after a struggle with loss;
- to develop self-confidence;
- to keep a long-term perspective and consider the stressful event in a broader context;
- to maintain a hopeful outlook, expecting good things and visualizing what is wished;
- to take care of one's mind and body, exercising regularly, paying attention to one's own needs and feelings and engaging in relaxing activities that one enjoys.
- to learn from the past

- to maintain flexibility and balance in life

In the research (Schnurr et alia, 2004), Japanese ancestry Americans had only 14% of the incidence of PTSD that European ancestry Americans had. That beats any PTSD treatment success rate! Polynesian (in the research, specifically Hawaiian; in many ways the same culture as New Zealand Maori or Samoan) ancestry also reduced PTSD rates to 35%. Resilience is pretty much the core successful human response to disaster that NLP seeks to remedially create (in fact NLP goal-setting, reframing and dissociation are all listed in the 10 points above). Note that research show that resilience is not a set personality trait so much as a set of actions you can choose to take. Also note that in the same research, a past history of being a survivor of violence almost doubles the risk of PTSD (177%). Good relationships buffer us from harm, bad ones signal a need for extra support.

Patterns of Chronicity

The thinking styles that obstruct change and recovery after a traumatic event are of course ones that were learned earlier in a person's life. The simplest way to deal with them is to show the person how they are operating and have them practice an alternative. It's not very glamorous compared to ten years of psychotherapy, but it's a lot cheaper. NLP Trainer Andy Austin lists several of these "patterns of chronicity" and here we have adapted his categories as a reminder.

The Big "What If…" Question. "Yes, but, what if… which means…(an impossible to manage scenario)?" The positive intention of negative "What if?" questions is to attempt to anticipate and find solutions to future challenges, but by running it on impossible scenarios, the person is locked in panic. Happy people don't spend all day asking "What if I die horribly?"

The Big "Why…?" Question. "Why did this happen to me?" The positive intention of past-related "Why?" questions is to find new meanings, but the person rejects each possible future-oriented meaning and keeps searching as if trying to find a meaning which can change the traumatic event or recreate the past.

The Big Maybe Response. When asked to scale their current experience of an emotion, or give any report on their internal experience, the person says they are not sure, or prefaces their answer with "Maybe". The positive intention of "Maybe" responses is to avoid mistakes such as false hope, but by refusing to commit to any specific data, the person can never measure change and can never experience success.

Testing for Existence of The Problem Rather Than Testing for Change. Even though 99% improvement might be made, if the person with chronicity is able to locate just 1% of the problem existing, this will generally be seen as representative of 100% of the problem existing. The positive intention of "Can I still do it?" responses is to detect and respond to danger effectively, but by failing to notice improvement the person continuously reinstalls the entire problem.

Negative Nominalisations. The person talks about their traumatic responses as if they were "things" rather than actions. "I have Trauma", "I have PTSD", "I have a Wounded Inner Child", "I have a Clinical Depression.". The positive intention of Negative Nominalisations is to explain what is happening by labelling it, but the result is that the processes being discussed seem permanent, damaged and even become personified as malevolent, and so are unable to be simply changed.

Being "At Effect" rather than "Being At Cause". By being "at effect" the person experiences emotional problems happening to them, rather than being something that happens by them. A person "at effect" will seek treatment rather than seek change. Questions such as "Will this work for me?" or statements such as "It didn't work for me." And "It worked for a day and then the problem came back." Presuppose that the problem and the NLP process are 100% responsible and the person themselves is 0% responsible for their own results. The positive intention of "At Effect" responses is to explain what is happening without being at fault, but by not allowing for the possibility of their responses affecting their internal experience, the person makes it impossible to change their experience.

Anchoring In Social Change Movements

Breaking these patterns of chronicity is essential to your survival as a change agent. It involves learning to use the reframing we discussed previously. And it involves using anchoring carefully.

Summarising his study of a number of successful social change processes, New Zealand Community worker Ewen Derrick urges activists "Look after your own needs. If you are working and dealing with alienation, you too will attract some of the barnacles. Make sure you have a professional support group and someone you respect and relate to and with whom you can discuss events, progress, your own needs.... Take time off regularly. Go somewhere else than places you identify with your work. Attend events that strengthen your own cultural and spiritual resources.... The importance of celebration should never be overlooked by the community worker. No matter how small the victory the group should gather to share food, drink and song." (Derrick, 1982, p 118-119). Derrick is discussing here the intentional anchoring of positive states, and the feelings that are already associated with ones culture and spirituality, in order to clear the less pleasant anchors of working with alienation and dis-empowerment. NLP provides a very explicit way to do that, as demonstrated above.

In discussions with the French government about their Pacific nuclear tests, New Zealand activist Kate Dewes played a pivotal role outside of the government officialdom. She explains "Another example of our complementary roles was when the French refused to budge on wording in the final document in relation to the degree of international opposition to their nuclear testing. Our diplomats were extremely frustrated with the blocking tactics being used by certain officials. One evening the NZ delegation was socialising with the Western diplomats and a French diplomat asked me to dance. I jokingly refused until he would agree to help establish an independent international scientific and medical inspection team to go to Mururoa to assess damage from the tests: something the international peace movement had promoted for many years. Finally he conceded and we danced briefly and talked about our daughters and their future in a world with nuclear weapons. He left promising to show me a photo of his daughters the next day. On arrival at the Mission the next morning, I was infuriated to read in the cables that France had detonated two nuclear bombs at Mururoa overnight. Determined to confront him I headed straight for the UN where we had a long and passionate exchange. I challenged him to read about women giving birth to jelly-fish babies in the booklet Pacific Women Speak, to share it with his wife and to search his conscience. He was visibly moved, and grudgingly agreed to speak with his delegation about changing the wording in the final document. When I reported this back to our Ambassador he was overjoyed and asked me to join the Ministry. On reflection, it was the freedom to summon the moral authority of motherhood, and speak strongly with no fear of losing a job or embarrassing my country, that facilitated this change." (Dewes, 1998)

Here, Dewes has invited the French diplomat to access the experience of being a parent. Anchored into that position, he then re-views the situation, and changes what he does. Dewes has anchored him back into a very simple state; the state of parental love. Bell Hooks, born Gloria Watkins, is an African American feminist and anti-racism activist who has embraced Buddhism as a way of bringing a "certain quality of mindfulness and stillness" to her life as a social change worker (ie, as a method of anchoring stillness). She says "In this society there is no powerful discourse on love emerging either from politically progressive radicals or from the left.... The absence of a sustained focus on love in progressive circles arises from a collective failure to acknowledge the needs of the spirit and an overdetermined emphasis on material concerns. Without love, our efforts to liberate ourselves and our world community from oppression and exploitation are doomed." (Quoted in Walljasper et alia, 2001, p 118). French revolutionary Daniel Cohn-Bendit emphasizes it on the final page of his report on the 1968 French revolutionary uprising by saying: "Reader, you have come to the end of this book, a book that wants to say only one thing: between us we can change this rotten society. Now, put on your coat and make for the nearest cinema. Look at their deadly lovemaking on the screen. Isn't it better in real life? Make up your mind to learn to love." (Cohn-Bendit, 2000, p 231).

At some time you have felt that love, and you have known in that moment that a society based on love is your birthright. Anchoring is a way to remind yourself of the joy of that realization at every moment of your work. It is a way to make that revolutionary society begin now, in you. Cohn-Bendit concludes: "Stay awhile in the street. Look at the passers-by and remind yourself: the last word has not yet been said. Then act. Act with others, not for them. Make the revolution here and now. It is your own. *C'est pour toi que tu fais la révolution.*" (Cohn-Bendit, 2000, p 231). It is for you, yourself, that you make the revolution!

Creating Relationships That Survive

Social activism focuses us on what we disagree with, and this is not a smart filter to bring home into our intimate relationships. The survival of those relationships is an important part of how we maintain our resilience and human-ness as change agents. If we can't even create a single loving relationship with our friend or partner, how do we imagine that we can create a more cooperative world? In this chapter I want to review what we know from research about how to create friendships that survive challenging times.

It's no secret that one to one intimate relationships (such as marriage) are more challenging to maintain in the world today. In the United States, for example, between 50% and 67% of first marriages end in divorce, and the percentage is higher for each subsequent marriage and higher for non-marital intimate partnerships. One sad result of this is increased illness. Those of us who are able to stay in an intimate couple (whether we are male or female) will live approximately 4 years longer, making the couples lifestyle one of the most significant life extension interventions known (Gottman and Silver, 1999, p 4). The cost of separation in economic terms is the source of many jokes, but it is also a realistic fact that people who separate, after living together for any length of time, considerably affect their financial future.

The Gottman Revolution In Couples Counselling

Seattle's Washington University researchers and marital therapists John and Julie Gottman have been in the forefront of a revolution in couples work. Their in depth research on more than a thousand couples over the last thirty years has debunked many cherished theories about what makes intimate relationships work. It has shown, for example, that in general the personality characteristics and even the objective degree of similarity between the couple's personality types is irrelevant to marital happiness. Even the number of arguments between the couple does not determine a couple's sense of satisfaction and likelihood of separation. However, in happy couples, each person perceives the other as being basically a functional person (with certain quirks) and basically similar to them. In happy couples, each perceives arguments as useful and manageable expressions of differences. In unhappy relationships, each partner perceives the other as basically flawed and unlike them, and conflicts are experienced as emotionally traumatic (Gottman, 1999, p 19-21).

When couples are videotaped 24 hours a day, the difference between happy couples and unhappy couples is very small – for example it includes happy couples saying approximately 100 more words of positive comment per day (a mere 30 seconds more of positive talking) compared to unhappy couples. But those 30 seconds are crucial (Gottman, 1999, p 59). Furthermore there are subtle differences in the linguistic patterns that successful couples use before, during and after an argument. These differences in linguistic patterns pervade the whole relationship though, not just the arguments. Gottman's researchers have shown that they can accurately predict whether a couple will divorce just by listening to a five minute conversation between the couple, by identifying the specific language patterns used and seeing the specific non-verbal responses they make to each other (Gottman and Silver, 1999, p 3). They can predict whether a couple will be together twelve years later, and do so with 96% accuracy. But these detailed differences are not merely present in arguments. As Gottman says, his research has shown that "successful conflict resolution isn't what makes marriages succeed." (Gottman and Silver, 1999, p 11). The formation of an intimate relationship, Gottman's research shows, is the formation of a whole new culture. It is the quality of the friendship between the couple, as evidenced in their exact verbal and non-verbal communication, which counts, for both men and women.

Gottman says "In my therapy the entire problem-solving process is recast as one of identifying and harmonizing people's basic life dreams. Much of the process of conflict resolution is an exploration in using the marital friendship to help make one another's life dreams come true." (Gottman, 1999, p 184).

Clear Problem Ownership

I train instructors of a process for creating cooperative relationships. This process, called Transforming Communication, is explained in more depth in several other books, and here I want to quickly give you the basics.

To begin using the methodology of Transforming Communication in any relationship situation, one simply checks whether at this moment one's own present internal state is desired or not (a "problem", as NLP trainer Robert Dilts notes in Dilts, 1993, p193, is any distance between present state and desired state). One then steps into what NLP calls "second position" and checks whether the other person's internal state is desired by them or not. There are four possible results to these checks (Gordon, 1974, p38-39):

1) Neither of us owns a Problem. If both states are desired, then no problem exists, and the focus of communication can be towards individual and mutual enjoyment. In the situation where neither of us owns a problem, a larger range of language patterns will be safe to use (safe in the sense of preserving both of our self esteem, and preserving the relationship). This area offers the most potential for us to grow personally, as each of us has energy free from problem-solving to focus on our goals and on discovery. It is the area where a couple build their "positive emotional bank account" that they may need to draw on in conflict resolution. Gottman's research shows that successful couples devote approximately 20 minutes a day to non-problem activities such as:

- Simply responding to each comment or nonverbal communication by their partner. Such communications are called "bids" (for attention or caring) by John Gottman and in a healthy relationship most bids are responded to. Either cooperation or disagreement are indications of a successful bid, but in unhappy couples over 50% of bids are not even detected by the partner (Gottman, 1999, p 201)
- Making positive and appreciative comments about the relationship. The ratio of positive comments to negative comments in successful relationships is approximately 5 to 1, whereas in unsuccessful relationships it is less than 1 to 1. This is true both in conflict and in everyday interaction (Gottman, 1999, p 59-61). Indeed, Gottman found that in successful relationships, participants (women in particular) tended to monitor and limit the quantity of negative comments by their partners about anything at all. In unsuccessful relationships, they accepted that their partner had a right to be continuously and unproductively angry, unhappy and blaming of both them and others (Gottman, 1999, p 73-74) .
- Discussing each person's values and dreams, and finding shared values and creating shared meanings. Reviewing the history of their relationship and reframing it as a positive story of friendship.
- Sharing meals together, and sharing housework together. Going out together, both for practical purposes such as shopping, and for entertainment
- Checking in after time apart and each listening to each other's story.

If one of the people is in an undesired state, then they "own a problem" in the terms first used by Dr Thomas Gordon (1955). This does not mean that they are "at fault" or "should" change something. It simply means that they are not in their desired state. Possible results 2), 3), and 4) relate to this situation.

2) The other person owns a problem. If I am in a relationship where at this moment I feel okay, and the other person does not (i.e. they are in an undesired or "problem" state), it can be useful to focus my attention on assisting them to reach their desired state. This process occurs when you are listening to your spouse talking about a difficult day, or when you offer to assist your co-worker to learn how to perform a new work task. The most effective skills for Helping will be ones that linguistically identify the problem space and the desired state as existing inside the other person's experience (I will say, for example, "So what you want to change is..." rather than "So what I think you should change is..."). These skills avoid patronising the person by suggesting what they "should" aim for, "should" feel and "should" be able to cope with. These skills include:

- Non-verbal rapport. Gottman's research demonstrates the power of what NLP calls matching and mirroring. Couples who can understand each other actually adjust their bodies to experience what the other person is experiencing. They breathe in time with each other, sit in similar positions, use similar voice tonality, and even their heart rates match (Gottman, 1999, p 27). We discussed this under the heading "Rapport" in an earlier chapter.
- Open questions that invite the other person to talk. These usually begin with the words "How...?" and "What...?" rather than the more intrusive "Why...?" or the more leading "Did you...?", "Didn't you...?" and "Don't you...?"
- Reflective listening. This involves restating the person's own experience, opinions and feelings, in words which are similar to theirs e.g. "That was an unpleasant experience then." "You wanted to get a different perspective." In this situation in particular (where the other partner owns a problem), Gottman's research identified that reflective listening was the most powerful response offered by members of successful relationships (Gottman and Silver, 1999, p 87-89.

3) I own a problem. If I am in a relationship where at this moment the other person feels okay, and I do not (i.e. I am in an undesired or "problem" state), it can be useful to focus my attention on finding a way for me to reach my desired state. This process could be called Problem Solving. As we know in NLP, people own a problem in response to particular internal representations. If the representations related to my problem state are about the other person (if I'm upset or angry or hurt "about something they did", for example) then this process of problem solving is called Assertion. For example, I own a problem where I'm frustrated about my spouse's failure to wash the dishes, or where I'm resentful that I ended up doing extra work when my partner didn't arrive home on time. The most effective skill for Assertion will be one that linguistically identifies the problem and the desired state as existing inside my own experience ("What I want to change is..." rather than "So what you might want to do is..."). This skill is called an "I message" (Gordon, 1974, 139-145). In a conflict, a clear I message identifies:

- the sensory specific behaviour that is the subject of the concern,
- the internal state (emotion) which I have generated in response to this behaviour,
- any sensory specific effects on me of that behaviour.

An example of the format for an I message would be "When...[sensory specific behaviour], I feel...[congruent description of my internal state] and the effect on me is... [sensory specific effects of the behaviour]". This structure avoids insulting or blaming the other person, and avoids patronising them by telling them what they "should" do. By not suggesting one specific solution, it leaves the process of generating solutions until the other person's situation has been heard and can be taken into account (as in examples below). Helping skills by themselves will be ineffective in the area where I own a problem, suggesting to the other person that it's up to them what solution is reached.

Generally, it is important to understand that I messages are a gentle start-up to a discussion that can resolve your problem, rather than intended to be a "final word" that solves the problem. Often when you send an I message you will discover that the other person is not happy to change because they themselves have some other opinion or some other problem.

4) We both own a problem. This situation implies that some combination of linguistic skills will be useful (So what you want is... and what I want is...). Where we both own a problem in response to related internal representations, then this situation is a "Conflict". This doesn't mean that we are necessarily opposed to each other, or that one of us must win and one lose. It simply means that we both are upset, angry, hurt etc about related issues (e.g. I think we should spend more time together and the other person wants more space. I want to use the family car tomorrow and so does my partner) Such situations benefit from a combination of the helping and assertive skills, as well as from specific conflict resolution skills (including win-win conflict resolution, consulting and modelling).

John Gottman's research reveals that successful couples differ not merely in their handling of conflicts, but in their handling of each of these four Problem Ownership areas. That means that effective coaching of couples needs to teach the couple to respond differently in each of the four areas also (Gottman, 1999, p 59-61).

Effectively Raising A Concern

The situation would be very easy if problem ownership stayed constant throughout any conversation. If this was the case, in the "no-problem" situation, a conversation would involve simply exploring positive states and outcomes together. In the "other owns a problem" situation, a conversation would involve simply pacing the other person's dilemma, assisting the other person to clarify what their outcome is, and guiding them through processes to assist change towards that. In the "I own a problem" situation, a conversation would involve simply asserting my position and identifying the changes I want.

In real life, it is more useful if I continuously monitor the changing internal states of myself and the other person, and adjust my language use to best represent the shifts of problem ownership, many of which are of course a result of my own previous communications. For example, in the midst of helping my partner solve her or his problem, I may discover that I myself am uncomfortable with the way my partner insists that I listen to complaints about what goes wrong, and does not shift to an outcome (solution focused) frame. From using Helping skills ("So for you the problem is..." and "So what you want is...") I would then shift to using Assertive skills ("One thing I'm finding frustrating about the way you're talking is..." and "I'd find it easier to help if...").

Most particularly, once I have used an Assertive skill, a common outcome is for my partner to shift into the problem state themselves (to feel uncomfortable in response to my communication). When a person hears my I message "I resented the way you didn't get that report to me on time as we'd arranged. It involved me in a lot of extra work" it is rare for them to respond with congruent joy and enthusiasm to improve next time. If you think of times when someone has, however skilfully, asserted themselves with you in this way, you'll notice that you're more likely to experience feelings of embarrassment, discomfort, hurt, annoyance, and mismatching responses. That is to say, you're more likely to own a problem about the message, and possibly about the issue.

If I've used an I message (Assertion skill) and the other person owns a problem about that, the next step to getting my problem solved will be to shift back from Assertion, and help them solve their own problem. To do this, I simply use reflective listening (a Helping language pattern), to pace their concern (e.g. "You think I'm over-reacting..."). As NLP points out, there is no resistance, only a lack of rapport. Once the other person feels fully heard in their own problem state (evidenced usually by a nod of the head), then it becomes possible to restate my I message taking into account their comment. As they have now been heard, their "emotional temperature" is reduced, and they are more able to hear my concern and respond positively to it.

The process of resolving such a situation by alternating between I messages and reflective listening is called the two step" in Transforming Communication because it is like a dance. Here's how it might sound in practice, in a discussion where Joan is using the model in a concern with her work colleague, Frank (notice that if Frank knew the model, the process would be even more fluent, but Joan can use the model regardless of this):

Joan: Frank, I have a problem I'd like to discuss. You arrived home an hour later than expected a couple of times last week and I didn't get the time to myself in the evening that I was hoping for, and I guess I feel a bit resentful about spending that much of my day child-minding. [Joan "owns" a problem: she is the one who is concerned about what has happened, so she uses an I message. Frank is feeling Okay, so initially he doesn't own a problem.]

Frank: [sighs] Lighten up Joan. I had a busy day; that's all.

Joan: You think I'm over-reacting, and you had a lot of extra stuff to do. [Frank responds indicating that he owns a problem, so Joan does the Two Step and reflective listens him.]

Frank: [nods] Sure. And it's no big deal.

Joan: Well, I still want to know that I have time to myself to do the things that I really want to do. My day is long too. [Frank's nod indicates he feels paced/understood, so Joan Two Steps and restates her I message.]

Frank: Look, I guess I just forgot how important this can be to you. I'll be more careful. How about, if I do arrive late in future, I could adjust later and give you extra time on the weekend.

Joan: Thanks. I would appreciate your help with that.

Frank: Okay. I just wasn't thinking. Sorry. [Frank is now apologising. As he's still not feeling totally comfortable, Joan again acknowledges his comments before thanking him for changing his approach.]

Joan: Well I'd appreciate sort of knowing that the time for myself is there. Thanks.

This, of course, is a "best case" scenario. There are two other possible outcomes of this discussion, described below. Both are "conflicts".

John Gottman found that such discussions and conflicts occurred in even the best relationships, and that effective couples might get very emotional (even angry) as they talked about such issues, but they avoided certain key destructive behaviours. Those seven core behaviours to avoid (listed by Gottman and Silver, 1999, p 25-46) include:

- Harsh Start-up of the discussion with an angrily stated "You message"
- Criticism of the person as a person rather than complaint about their behaviour.
- Contempt of the other person, conveyed nonverbally by raised eyebrows and a sneering facial expression, or verbally by mockery of the person's position, sarcasm and hostile humour. This is the most serious of the seven behaviours, it is the fastest way to predict separation, and it is virtually unseen in successful relationships (Gottman, 1999, p 128)
- Defensiveness, expressed by arguing/blaming back while refusing to acknowledge the other's concern or accept that they have a problem.
- Stonewalling, expressed by simply stopping talking without negotiating, or leaving the room.
- Becoming Emotionally Flooded, as a result of these behaviours, as evidenced by the person being physically over-aroused, with a pulse above 95 beats per minute.
- Failure of Repair Attempts and Self-nurturing behaviours, e.g. to call a halt for time to calm down, or to apologise and ask to start again, as these last patterns occur.

Three Types Of Conflict

The Two Step process will lead to one of three outcomes. Depending on which outcome occurs, you can easily identify which steps to take next to most effectively resolve the conflict.

Outcome 1) Misunderstanding. The Two Step process itself resolves the conflict (as above). Such conflict could be considered a simple miscommunication. In the example above, for instance, once Frank has clearly heard what Joan's problem is (which is assisted by her use of I messages and reflective listening) the problem is solved. No further action may be needed.

Outcome 2) Conflict of Needs. As a result of the Two Step process, it becomes clear that both people have a concrete problem. Both people can understand that the other person has a problem, though they are reluctant to solve the other person's problem as this would leave them with their own difficulty. Thomas Gordon calls this a Conflict of Needs. In NLP terms it is a conflict which both parties have agreed to keep at the neurological level of environment, behaviour or capability (their values and sense of identity are not a subject of discussion, only how and where they do what). John Gottman calls this a "Solvable Conflict" and recommends developing solutions which honour both parties "dreams" in the conflict. In such a situation, Gordon recommends the skilled use of his 6 step win-win conflict resolution model (Gordon, 1974, p217-234). Gordon's six steps are:

1. Identify the problem in terms of two sets of needs, rather than two conflicting solutions. Needs are more general descriptions than solutions ("How will you know that this problem is solved?" or "If you get this solution, what do you get through that, that is even more important?" rather than "What specific way would you suggest to solve this problem right now?"). Gottman describes this as discovering what the "dreams" behind the stated solution are.
2. Brainstorm potential solutions which could meet both sets of needs/outcomes/dreams.
3. Evaluate the ability of these proposed solutions to meet both sets of needs.
4. Choose a solution or more than one solutions to put into action.
5. Act
6. Evaluate the results.

An example would be if the conversation between Frank and Joan went like this:

Joan: Frank, I have a problem I'd like to discuss. You arrived home an hour later than expected a couple of times last week and I didn't get the time to myself in the evening that I was hoping for, and I guess I feel a bit resentful about spending that much of my day child-minding. [Joan "owns" a problem: she is the one who is concerned about what has happened, so she uses an I message. Frank is feeling Okay, so initially he doesn't own a problem.]
Frank: [sighs] Lighten up Joan. I had a busy day; that's all.
Joan: You think I'm over-reacting, and you had a lot of extra stuff to do. [Frank responds indicating that he owns a problem, so Joan does the Two Step and reflective listens him.]
Frank: [nods] Sure. And if I come home without completing that stuff, I'll end up in rouble at work.
Joan: So you want to make sure you get the things done at work that are your responsibility. Well, I still want to know that I have time to myself to do the things that I really want to do. My day is long too.

Maybe we can find a way to meet both those concerns. [Frank now understands that Joan has a concrete problem, as his nod indicates, but if he agreed to help her, he'd have a problem of his own (trying to guess what issues were serious enough for her). This is what Thomas Gordon calls a Conflict of Needs and John Gottman calls a solvable problem. Joan sums up the two sets of needs/outcomes, and invites Frank to begin win-win conflict resolution to identify a solution which will meet both sets of needs/outcomes.]

Frank. [nods] Yeah. I guess I could adjust later and give you extra time on the weekend if I get home late in the week.

Joan: Thanks. That would work for me too. I would appreciate your help with that.

Frank: Okay. Let's do that.

Outcome 3) Conflict of Values. As a result of the Two Step process, it becomes clear that at least one person believes that the conflict involves their deeper beliefs, values or sense of identity. In Robert Dilts' NLP model these are disagreements at a higher neurological level (Dilts, 1993, p 55-56). Such a person will be reluctant to engage in the sort of conflict resolution demonstrated above because their values are "non-negotiable". Put another way, Person A believes that Person B is trying to change Person A's values/identity, which Person A considers is really "none of Person B's business". This is what Thomas Gordon calls a "Values Conflict" (Gordon, 1974, p283-306). Note that in this situation it is less likely that a satisfactory solution will be reached in one session.

John Gottman found that 69% of all relationship conflicts were in this category, in both successful and unsuccessful relationships (Gottman and Silver, 1999, p 130). Gottman calls these conflicts "unsolvable problems", where the partners' basic dreams are in conflict. He doesn't mean that nothing can be done about such conflicts; simply that they cannot be resolved in a session of "problem-solving" talk. In fact, he notes that successful couples learn to respect and honour each other's differing values, and accept that the difference will continue for some time.

Thomas Gordon also recommends that many values conflicts are best dealt with by learning to live with the difference, or to altering the relationship so that the other person's values do not clash so frequently with theirs. Skills that are recommended by Thomas Gordon for actually influencing others values include values consulting, and modelling. Modelling involves demonstrating, in one's own behaviour, the effectiveness of one's values. Values consulting is a skilled linguistic influencing process which requires (Gordon, 1974, p294-297):

1. Ensuring you have been "hired" as a consultant (that the other person agrees to listen).
2. Preparing your case, especially any relevant information.
3. Sharing your expertise and opinions in simple I message form ("I believe...") and shifting gears to active listen the other's opinion.
4. Leaving the other to make up their own mind, rather than attempting to force a new value. People rarely change values in direct interaction with someone who shares the opposing value. It is more common for them to change at a later time, having been left in a positive state, to choose.

If you attempted to resolve Conflicts of Values as if they were Conflicts of Needs, it could well lead to disillusionment with the conflict resolution process, and the belief that "some people just cannot be engaged in a win-win conflict resolution way". Here's how the conversation between Frank and Joan might go if it was a Conflict of Values:

Joan: Frank, I have a problem I'd like to discuss. You arrived home an hour later than expected a couple of times last week and I didn't get the time to myself in the evening that I was hoping for, and I guess I feel a bit resentful about spending that much of my day child-minding. [Joan "owns" a problem: she is the one who is concerned about what has happened, so she uses an I message. Frank is feeling Okay, so initially he doesn't own a problem.]

Frank: [sighs] Lighten up Joan. I had a busy day; that's all.

Joan: You think I'm over-reacting, and you had a lot of extra stuff to do. [Frank responds indicating that he owns a problem, so Joan does the Two Step and reflective listens him.]

Frank: [nods] Sure. I mean, that's my life. My work is also important to me. I don't really feel comfortable negotiating that with you. [Frank identifies a difference in values about the issue]

Joan: So you see that as your life to decide about. Well, I have a different way of thinking about that particular part of it – the timing piece. I'd like to discuss it some more some time. Would you be willing to hear my thoughts about that? [Joan reflective listens Frank's value and identifies the difference.]

Frank: [sighs] Maybe.... Yeah, I guess so. I don't want to get into a heavy discussion about it now though.

Joan: Great. How about the kids are out on Saturday: maybe we could put aside half an hour to clarify our approaches with each other. [Joan arranges to meet with Frank at a time that is easier for him to discuss their values difference. There, she will continue to use reflective listening and I messages to advocate her value, acting as what Thomas Gordon calls a "Values Consultant", and modelling her values.]

Frank: Okay; that'll work.

The Two Step: Three Results Of I Messages

Here's another example, shown graphically. Imagine that Jane is a teenager who gets up late in the morning. Her father, Jack, finds that this results in him having less time to tidy up before he leaves for work.He decides to send an I message to explain his problem. In the diagrams, when Jack sends his I message, we will have him symbolically move out of rapport by stepping down the page. When Jane feels understood as a result of Jack's reflecting, we will have her move down the page back into rapport. This is a kind of "dance" that I call the "Two Step".

1. Jane agrees congruently to change to solve Jack's problem.

2. Jane and Jack identify that they both own a problem. While Jane can understand that their behaviour concretely affects Jack, she is not willing to change because it would cause *her* a problem. (Conflict of Needs)

3. Jane considers this matter to be "none of Jack's business". Jane is thus not willing to negotiate the issue. (Conflict of Values)

A 4th Possibility?

In some cultures (Japan and New Zealand are examples) conflict is avoided and the other person may not be willing to explain their challenge, and will hide their situation. This is far less common in European cultures. While the other can understand that their behaviour concretely affects you, they are not willing to change because change would create a challenge for them, **and** also they are not comfortable explaining this. The result is that the other superficially agrees, but fails to change their behaviour. This needs a little more care to find out what the other person's needs actually are so you can begin to think up solutions that will meet them and motivate the person to cooperate. (Hidden Conflict of Needs)

Any of these three outcomes is a successful result of sending the I message and reflective listening.

Creating Cooperative Relationships At Home Versus Political Action

Once you understand this model of Problem Ownership and the Two Step, then you understand that your interactions as a Political Activist are generally in a very specific part of the relationship model - you have a conflict of values with those in power. Rather than thinking of these skills as just a way of sustaining your private relationships, in the next chapter we will focus in on how to use them to influence society.

To summarise:

No Problem area: Build positive experiences.	Other Person Owns A Problem: Use Reflective listening.
I Own A Problem: Use sensory specific I messages and listen to the response.	Both Of Us Own A Problem (Conflict). Use the win-win method, or in values conflicts use Consulting and Modelling

How Do Activists *Influence* Society?

Coercion or Influencing Values?

Now that you understand the Transforming Communication model, you can see that as an activist, you "own a problem" (there's something you want to change) and your aim is usually to change someone else's **values.** This is the most challenging part of any relationship, and yet of course the most potentially transformative part. I need to be frank with you: sometimes you would decide that you will do whatever you can to force them to do what you think they should. This process of "non-violent coercion" is what boycotts, strikes, sit-ins and political revolutions achieve. You need to understand two things about these tactics before you use them, though. Firstly, they do not convince the other person that you are right - at best they convince the other person that you cannot be controlled, cannot be stopped. They may create obedience, but they do not create cooperation. If the people you coerced later discover a way they can stop you, they will, and all the more forcefully because they know you used coercion against them. This is why counter-revolution is such an issue after major social change. Secondly, then, you need to maintain your coercion indefinitely. As writer Samuel Butler said, "He who agrees against his will... is of the same opinion still." (quoted in Cialdini, 1993, p 80). None-the-less, Mahatma Gandhi himself was very clear that sometimes he was using coercion to get his results.

Non-violent protest researcher and theorist Gene Sharp suggests that non-violent protest actions can succeed by three different mechanisms.

1. **Non-violent Coercion.** The February 1917 Revolution in Russia is a famous example of this. A general strike simply paralysed the country and the Tsar was unable to act, effectively transferring power to the provisional parliamentary government and the workers councils (the soviets). Although the Tsar was later to be executed, the handover of state power itself was coercive but non-violent.
2. **Accommodation.** Sharp defines accommodation as the situation when the influenced party/government adjusts its policies to avoid the nuisance value of protests. In 1957, for example, black South African workers boycotted their apartheid era buses to protest a price rise. It was white business leaders who pressured the government to subsidise the bus charges, because of their problems coping with workers arriving exhausted after long walks. While not actually coerced into change, the business leaders were also not fully converted to the black cause. They merely found it expedient to change their policy.

3. **Conversion.** Of course, this is the ideal of non-violence. Sharp quotes Mahatma Gandhi as saying to the British viceroy "For my ambition is no less than to convert the British people through non-violence, and thus make them see the wrong they have done to India." (Sharp, 1973, p 707). The aim here is actually to change the minds of the other people so that they empathise with and agree with you.

I will review each of the main choices, using Gene Sharps' listing.

1) Using *Coercive Power* In Values Conflicts

In the real world there are some situations (either conflicts of needs or conflicts of values) where you will decide it's worth the damage to control another person's behaviour by using power (ie by using coercion, rewards and punishments). Thomas Gordon suggests (Gordon, 1974, p279-282) that these situations could include:

- Situations where you don't have the say over what the rule is. If you work for a company you won't be able to negotiate solutions that give away their property, even though these solutions may have no concrete effect on you personally. If you are a teacher you won't be able to arrange for someone to break a school rule. (You can, of course, work to change such rules.)
- Situations where your own need is overriding. You don't, for instance, have to put up with a person hitting you; forcibly preventing them may well be worth their response of frustration or resentment.
- Situations where it seems to you that another person is obviously in danger. It wouldn't make sense to calmly watch someone walk in front of a speeding car, while sending the clear I message "I'm really worried that that car will hit you!" Mostly their initial annoyance, at being grabbed and pulled off the road, will be worth coping with.
- Situations where there is no time to discuss the matter. If you have a conflict arise ten minutes before your plane is due to take off, you may decide it's worth temporarily refusing to sort it out.
- Situations where talking rationally with the person is impossible. This will include many conflicts involving children less than two years old, and conflicts with people who are drunk or fully unconnected to reality.

The most obvious example of using power in a values conflict is a decision to prevent one person harming another. Of course, if you saw one person about to injure another, and you knew you could immediately stop them, you may decide it is worth using your power to do so, even though this is clearly "just" a values conflict. Even in these cases, it's worth remembering the damage power over others causes. You can reduce the damage to your relationship by:

- Only using the minimum force needed to solve your problem.
- Explaining, afterwards, how you came to use power, and assuring the other person that this is not your usual intention.
- Using reflective listening to acknowledge their resentment, and spending time rebuilding your relationship.
- Planning how to avoid that situation in future.

These last three steps could be done quite simply, as in this example: "I'd like to talk about what happened before. I don't mean to push you around, and only acted the way I did because I couldn't find a way to safely sort it out at the time. I guess you felt pretty annoyed, and I'd like to try and sort out some agreement, so we don't get into that situation again."

This is an emergency strategy for times when the use of power was logically unavoidable (rather than times when it seemed like a simple solution). To restate the case, the use of coercion in relationships is associated consistently with destructive effects for both participants and for the relationship (see Bolstad, 2004).

2) Using Conflict Resolution To Create Values *Accommodation*

In a conflict of needs each person can understand that their behaviours affect the other person. The whole focus of discussion is then about how to arrange what happens so that the undesired effects do not happen. You could treat the behaviour within even serious values conflicts this way.

Let's take an example. I may disapprove of you saying the word "God" casually, because I believe that this is "blasphemy" and insults something that is sacred to me. If you usually say this word as a casual expletive and as a curse when you are annoyed, you may think that it is none of my business. After all, it doesn't have any concrete effect on me for you to say a word. It doesn't cause me to bleed from the mouth or to lose money or have to do extra work. If I attempted to resolve the whole Values collisions as if it was a Conflict of Needs, you may get quite angry at my intruding into your psychological "territory". This could well lead to me being disillusioned with the conflict resolution process, and believing that "some people just cannot be engaged in win-win conflict resolution".

However, I might agree with you that your lack of value for the word "God" is your own business, and yet ask you to agree not to say that word casually when I'm around you. I would be acknowledging that your value would stay the same, but asking you to change a part of the behaviour which happens around me. Or I might explain that when you are frustrated or angry, I will choose not to be around you, and ask that you understand this as a form of spiritual self-protection. At first, these solutions seem like win-win solutions which could solve the problem. After all, you get to keep your value and I get to protect myself from it. In reality though, this is risky. You may become hurt that I avoid you when you are frustrated. You may begin to feel that you are not being true to yourself by holding back from saying "God" when around me. You may eventually suspect that our "agreement" is really a way of pressuring you to change. In this case you are *accommodating* my concern, not being fully coerced into respecting it, but definitely not being converted by it.

3) Using Influencing Skills To *"Convert"* The Other Person

There are three key influencing skills that social activists like Amory Lovins (see below) use to persuade even large businesses to change their values. These three skills can also be used in individual relationships, at home as well as with work clients and colleagues. They can even be used politically between nations states or communities. And most interestingly, you already have experiences where they have worked when other people have used them with you. Think of a time that you changed your own values, beliefs or ways of doing things, due to the influence of another person (a teacher, a friend, a mentor, or even someone that you read a book by). Chances are that there were three factors involved in your change.

1. The person influencing you shared some other important values with you.
2. The person influencing you practiced what they preached, and you could see that their value worked for them.
3. The person influencing you explained their opinion respectfully and listened to or acknowledged your opinion.

I will call these three skills a) Utilising Shared Values, b) Modelling and c) Values Consulting.

Identifying Shared Values

It may seem strange to say that if you want to influence someone's values you need to start by finding a value you share, but its true. It's the same basic idea that we discussed when talking about rapport. People do not respond to calls for change from people who are totally different to them. The Search Conference model is a step by step methodology for guiding a group to the discovery of a co-operative future based on shared values. Rita Schweitz, for example, was the co-ordinator of a 1991 search conference on the use and quality of water from the upper Colorado river basin (Weisbord, 1992, p 215-228). This issue concerned local, municipal, state and national government organisations, water provider companies, agricultural and industrial water user companies, conservationists, first nations and recreational user groups. Decades of bitter values conflicts lay behind the issue. State agencies were involved in taking private firms to court over their use of water at the time. Now all these warring parties were together in one room. Enormous care needed to be taken to build rapport safely and set ground-rules on the first day of the conference, when several members arrived with their lawyers in tow!

Rita Schweitz and the other organisers were very careful to structure the process so that arguments didn't erupt and get out of hand at the meeting of 48 people. On the second day, when each "stakeholder group" presented its own perspective and the others listened, only reflective listening and clarifying questions were permitted. The atmosphere in the first part of the conference process was described by the organisers as one of pessimism and challenge, but all that changed when people's values in the area under discussion were listed. A dramatic collection of *shared* values emerged, including an attraction to the mountains, the outdoors and enjoyment of the quality of life in Colorado. Talking about these values, one participant made a heartfelt plea that it was "time to change our ways", and the whole conference seemed to nod together. The rapport built by this apparently irrelevant personal sharing inspired major changes in attitude. On the morning of the third day, as participants breakfasted together, one remarked to Schweitz, "This must be the paradigm shift people talk about." A collaborative decisionmaking structure was set up for future planning, progress was made towards legislative reform proposals, and a second conference was set for a year later.

A key tool in this process is listing values. In Neuro Linguistic Programming, there's a very simple process which assists people to create this sort of values list explicitly. First, you choose an area of your life, such as "relationships", "career", "personal growth" or simply life as a whole. Then you ask "What's important to me about this area?" and list all the words/phrases that come to mind. If you're uncertain, remember back to a time in your life when you were highly motivated towards that area of your life. Step into your body at that time and ask "What's important to me about this area now?"

Once you have a list of at least six things, check which thing is <u>most</u> important to you. Then ask, "If I have that thing, what is next most important from this list?" Continue till you have the whole list in order and then review your choices. Is number 1) really more important then number 2), or is number 2) more important than number 1)? Continue comparing each value to the ones next in the list until your list feels, looks, and sounds right. Have a look at that list. It's the most important decision making information you could ever have for that area of life. In exploring your values, you are identifying the deepest levels of motivation.

Utilising Shared Values

If you're trying to persuade someone to change their values, you can use this same principle. In New Zealand in the 1970s, the Health department discovered the risks of cigarette smoking, and mounted a campaign to discourage it. They explained that smoking increased the risk of early death. This motivated many middle aged people to stop, but left most teenagers unaffected. Living a long life is often not a high value of teenagers (because they assume they're going to live one anyway). In the 1980s, the government succeeded in reaching teenagers, by running a campaign suggesting that no-one would want to kiss someone who had just smoked a cigarette. They had identified a core value of most teenagers (being liked).

There was still a problem, though. In 1981, the rate of smoking amongst Maori women aged 15-44 was twice that of non-Maori (63% compared to 31%; see Pomare, 1988). Neither fear of death nor the need to be liked seemed to affect this group. Researchers discovered the key. What was the one thing that would make it worth Maori women giving up smoking? In 1994 I taught a large group of Maori women NLP techniques for smoking cessation, and it was immediately clear. All those present were motivated by the desire to care for their children and grandchildren. The Health Department found the same thing. A campaign based around this value led to the gradual lowering of the rate of smoking for Maori women. The first step was to find values that were shared by the group they wanted to influence.

In the book *Reframing*, NLP trainer Richard Bandler gives an interesting example of the use of shared values to resolve a conflict over non-shared values. A father has just told his daughter: "If you don't listen to me and don't come home by ten o'clock, I'll ground you for a week...". After checking that this message (a "you message" and a threat to use power) doesn't get a very good response from the daughter, Bandler asks the father what the *value* is behind his command. He replies: "Well, I care. I don't want her hanging out with hoods. I don't want her out in the street. There's dope out there. I want her to be in the house, safe and sound. She's my girl, and I want to make sure that she has the kind of experiences that she needs to grow up like I want her to grow up."

The daughter explains her values: 'But it's my life!' Bandler then points out a value that both of these people share. 'OK, Sam. Is part of that image that you have of your daughter growing up for her to be independent? Do you want her to be a woman who knows her own mind, who can stand on her own two feet and make decisions for herself based on the realities of the world? Or do you want her to be pushed around by other people's opinions?'

Once these two people realise that they share the value of 'independence', they will probably find more useful ways to behave. In a sense, they want the same thing, only their methods differ. The father may now be willing to alter his way of discussing the matter, the daughter may be willing to alter her evening pattern.

In May 2017, Daphne White interviewed linguist and political activist George Lakoff in the Berkeleyside online magazine*. She says "Lakoff's message is simple, but it is couched in the language of cognitive linguistics and neuroscience. The problem is that political candidates rely on pollsters and PR people, not linguists or neuroscientists. So when Lakoff repeatedly says that "voters don't vote their self-interest, they vote their values," progressive politicians continually ignore him." Lakoff explains that progressives need to identify the values that they share with conservatives, and explain progressive policies in terms of those values, not in terms of the progressives own values. Conservatives value protections and investments, he argues. "Every progressive knows that regulations are protections, but they don't say it," he adds. Similarly, "taxes" are actually "investments in public resources." But progressives need to frame their proposals inside these values. Lakoff predicted Donald Trump would win the 2017 USA election by getting 47% of the vote (he won with 46%).

*http://www.berkeleyside.com/2017/05/02/berkeley-author-george-lakoff-says-dont-underestimate-trump/

Utilizing shared values is the key pattern that we use in the "Citizens" role, which is the initial role used in raising an issue for change (see chapter 3, Social Change Styles and Rapport).

Values Consulting

A consultant is a person hired to offer their expert skills and knowledge. There are business consultants, educational consultants, health consultants, and so on. A consultant – client relationship is characterised by lateral rather than hierarchical interaction. The consultant cannot simply tell their client what to do, as a "line manager" could. They rely on their ability to persuade and convince.

You can use the consultant model to influence others' values. As an effective consultant:

1. Get prepared. Be well-informed about your subject. Don't bother trying to convince your kids about the dangers of drugs if they know more than you.
2. Don't start trying to influence until the other person has agreed to listen. (In other words, get yourself hired first.) The first statement of every good salesperson is a request to talk to you.
3. Explain your opinions using I messages in as brief a way as possible. By I messages, I'm not meaning full "When you... the effect on me is... and I feel..." I simply mean to say my opinion as an opinion ("I believe..."), rather than to say "You should..." or "The way the world is..."
4. Listen to the other person's opinions using reflective listening. Unless the person enjoys mismatching, assume in your reflective listening that they have positive intentions. Research suggests that even when this is not actually true, they will tend to respond positively to the assumption. Remember that "everyone believes that they are the good guy".
5. Leave the other person to make their own decision.

For example, in the following scenario, an educational consultant has recommended mind-mapping as a new form of note-taking. One student objects. Here's how the interaction goes when the consultant fails to use the above principles:

Consultant: I notice you're resisting that idea about the mind maps. Why?
Student: Well, I found it was taking a lot more time than normal notes do.
Consultant: Frankly, ten years from now, you'll wish you had picked up this idea.
Student: Yeah, well maybe. But I need to get the information now.
Consultant: I'm only telling you this to help you. You need to wise up a bit.
Student: Hey; lighten up. I think I'm doing OK.
Consultant: You'll be sorry. Pride comes before a fall, you know.

Student: What! I don't want to discuss this any more!
Consultant: Do you want to turn into a third rate learner? Is that your style?
Student: Fuck off

In this brief exchange, the consultant has been "fired". By trying to use increasing force, she has lost any ability to influence. The student begins to experience her as using her power over him, and his anger will prevent him cooperating in other areas of their relationship. It's by "consulting" like this that many parents get fired by their teenagers, many teachers get fired by their students, and many managers get fired by their team members. Here's how it could have been handled more effectively:

Consultant: I notice you haven't been using the mind-maps idea. Mind if I ask what happened?
Student: Well, I found it was taking a lot more time than normal notes do.
Consultant: So you needed to get things down quicker.
Student: Yeah. I could see the advantages in terms of getting the big picture, but...
Consultant: Well, that makes sense. In the long term, as I mentioned, large companies like Boeing suggests mind-maps can reduce the time needed to learn something to one tenth or less. I think it could speed things up later on. So whereas you thought mind-maps took more time, I think using mind maps could mean saving a lot of time.
Student: Maybe. I guess I had a sort of gut reaction that it felt weird.
Consultant: Right. It's a really different way of doing it. OK, thanks for listening anyway.
Student: Sure. I'll think it over. Maybe I was a little hasty.

This time, the result is quite different. Most important of all, the relationship between the consultant and the student is still intact. You can only influence someone who is willing to relate with you. Also, the student may well be about to change his value and use mind maps. Very few people change their values as you talk to them. Mostly, they need time to go away and think about it, imagine what the new value would be like, check how it feels and talk it over with themselves. If you leave them while they still feel good about you, they have a head start to feeling good about what you said.

Consulting is the key pattern that we use in the "Rebel" role, which is the second role used in raising an issue for change (see chapter 3, Social Change Styles and Rapport). Notice that effective consulting is also actually reframing (see chapter 4, Reframing).

Modelling

The third powerful skill for influencing someone's values is modelling. Modelling in this case simply means demonstrating, by your own actions, that what you value works. "Practise what you preach" may be a well-known saying, but it's fascinating how many people ignore this truth in their daily life. Teachers who routinely smoke in their staff room give out detentions to students caught smoking in the school toilets. Parents who make a practice of lying about their motives ("I'd like to give you a donation, but I have to go to the bank," "Sorry we can't come over to visit this Saturday, we have relatives coming," and so on) tell their kids not to lie. The very country which has defied United Nations resolutions and invaded Grenada, Panama and Nicaragua was most eager a year later to punish another country for invading Kuwait. A man who ends family arguments by punching his wife tells his kids to control their tempers.

If your values really work for you, others will be more likely to adopt them. This is particularly true if you have a good relationship with those people. People tend to copy the values of those they admire. Notice how often a husband and wife end up with similar opinions, or a group of friends all wear the same-style clothes. When a collection of much-admired rock musicians run a concert to aid famine victims, hundreds of thousands of their fans donate money. If you remember a teacher you really admired from earlier in your life, you can probably recall right now some of the ways you used that teacher as a model. Of course, the value does have to look appealing (ie it does have to work for you) if you want others to model it. A parent with a strong work ethic who comes home each night and talks about what a nightmare their job is does not excite their children to work as hard as they do.

Modelling is the key pattern that we use in the "Change Agent" role, which is the third role used in raising an issue for change (see chapter 3, Social Change Styles and Rapport).

Combining Consulting and Modelling: Metaphor

VitalSmarts is a business involved in influencing positive change around the world. Like Thomas Gordon, the VitalSmarts group start their search for influencing skills with the question: "How do people naturally change their values?" Their negative conclusion is very simple: people do *not* usually change as a result of rational arguments – in fact rational argument usually convinces people that their old view was correct. Their positive conclusion is also simple, and consistent with what we find when we ask people to remember great influencers: values or priorities (and thus values-laden behaviours) change when people have profound experiences where they model the new value from someone they can identify with. When they have that experience they need to believe that the change in behaviour will feel good to them (ie it will be valuable), and to believe that it will be possible for them to achieve.

The VitalSmarts group describe this process in terms of Albert Bandura's social modelling research, which was the source of the skill "Modelling", identified by Thomas Gordon for use in values conflicts. However the VitalSmarts team go an exciting step further and suggest that usually it is not possible to give people a direct modelled experience of the value being expressed (what standard TC modelling attempts to do) and so you need to "create profound vicarious experiences".

Some Examples: David Poindexter, Don Berwick, Jimmy Carter

Here are three examples of major values changes in the Health Care Industry, initiated by Erickson-style metaphorical communication, and discussed in the book *Influencers* (detailed information below comes from on-line sources mostly. The book *Influencers* is statistic-scarce).

David Poindexter is the founder of Population Communications International, which focuses on research on the use of entertainment to deliver pro-social messages aimed at improving the quality of life of audiences in the United States and abroad. During the decade of the 1970s, Poindexter was successful in mobilizing the producers and creators of numerous prime-time U.S. television shows, such as *Maude, All in the Family, The Mary Tyler Moore Show* and others, to incorporate discussions of family planning (birth control) and ending sexual stereotyping into the context of these shows. Starting in 1993, he and Martha Swai ran a radio drama called Twende na Wakati (Change with the Times) in Tanzania. The program dealt with AIDS transmission. Polling showed that the main male character, Mkwaju, was initially an attractive macho role model to male listeners. He was abusive to his wife, drank excessively, and had sex with prostitutes regularly. However, opinions shifted over the course of the program. As he died of AIDS, his wife, Tenu, made the decision to leave him, and set up her own successful business. By 1997 listenership of this program increased to an average of 66% country-wide, or almost two thirds of the adult population. 82% of listeners said they adopted a method of HIV/AIDS prevention as a direct result of listening to the programme; 25% of new family planning adopters in Tanzania cited *Twende Na Wakati* as the reason. The Dodoma area of Tanzania was excluded from radio transmission for this program in the years 1993-1995, as an experimental control. The ongoing tragedy in the Dodoma (where AIDS related behaviour did not change) resulted in this controlled part of the experiment being ended after two years in order to share the benefits the rest of the country received (Rogers and Singhal, 1999, p 131-134, and p 152-171).

The Professor of Paediatrics at Harvard Medical School, Don Berwick, began a campaign in 2004 to reduce the incidence of death from medical error, estimated to cost about 98,000 lives a year in the USA alone. Berwick set up the "Institute for Healthcare Improvement" and announced a goal to save 100,000 lives over the next 18 months. To do this, he chunked down to very specific goals such as reducing the number of "Adverse Drug Events" by 75% in a year. Extremely successful results are not achieved by rational argument, but by telling the people concerned moving stories of patients who died, often told by a person who experienced the event and who may even break down in tears as they tell the story. In June 2011 Berwick linked with Geraint Martin, CEO of Counties Manukau District Health Board (CMDHB) in Auckland, New Zealand to create the Ko Awatea programme, which provides Ericksonian-metaphor based training for 300 students a day. Inspired by IHI's Campaigns, Ko Awatea is running several campaigns of its own, the most ambitious of which is Saving 20,000 Bed Days with the goal to reduce hospital bed days by 5 percent.

Former President Jimmy Carter and former Nigerian President Dr. Yakubu Gowon were responsible for the eradication of an extremely distressing disease called Guinea Worm in Nigeria. The disease is spread by a tiny parasitic "worm" that lives in water and burrows under the person's skin, and its spread can only be stopped by meticulous filtering of all water before drinking. The disease symptoms include a fever and a desperate craving for water, which perpetuates the cycle of infection. Gowon, a much loved public figure in the country, went from village to village telling stories about how the disease had been eradicated in other villages and demonstrating the filtering process. When The Carter Center began spearheading the Guinea worm eradication campaign in 1986, an estimated 3.5 million cases were found in 20 countries in Africa and Asia. Nigeria was deemed the world's most Guinea worm–endemic country when the Nigerian Ministry of Health and The Carter Center began elimination efforts and conducted the first nationwide case search, resulting in 653,492 reported cases. The last case in Nigeria was suffered by Grace Otubu, 58, of Ezza Nkwubor village in Enugu state, whose case was cured in November 2008. There have been no cases since. Worldwide eradication continues and numbers of cases had dropped to 3,200 by December 2009

The Research On Metaphor: It's Rapport Again!

How does metaphor create this kind of influence? Greg Stephens, Lauren

Silbert and Uri Hasson at Princeton University (2010) first demonstrated that when one person tells a story and another person listens, the two people show synchronised brain activity. This rapport does not occur where mere facts are transmitted, and is probably due to the activation of sensory imagery evoked by the story in both teller and listener. They summarise "Verbal communication is a joint activity; however, speech production and comprehension have primarily been analyzed as independent processes within the boundaries of individual brains. Here, we applied fMRI to record brain activity from both speakers and listeners during natural verbal communication. We used the speaker's spatiotemporal brain activity to model listeners' brain activity and found that the speaker's activity is spatially and temporally coupled with the listener's activity. This coupling vanishes when participants fail to communicate. Moreover, though on average the listener's brain activity mirrors the speaker's activity with a delay, we also find areas that exhibit predictive anticipatory responses. We connected the extent of neural coupling to a quantitative measure of story comprehension and find that the greater the anticipatory speaker–listener coupling, the greater the understanding. We argue that the observed alignment of production- and comprehension-based processes serves as a mechanism by which brains convey information."

This confirms that in order to understand the story, the person imagines it in sensory detail, and thus synchronises with the story-teller, experiencing the emotional responses that the teller evokes as well. This is a very old understanding of course. When asked "Why do you speak to them in parables?" Jesus of Nazareth is said to have answered by quoting a Jewish prophet, saying that his aim was that people needed to be led through stories so "they should perceive with their eyes, and hear with their ears, and understand with their heart, and turn for me to heal them." (Christian Bible, Mathew, 13.15 More literally put in older translations, "so that those with eyes should see, those with ears should hear, and those with a heart turn to me and be healed.")

This research and the examples above emphasise that to be successful storytelling needs to meet the following criteria:

- Establish rapport first (eg note the respect that General Gowon was held in, the way people identified with Mkwaju in Tanzania).
- Tell stories with engaging sensory details, including emotion.
- Tell stories which reach a positive conclusion (eg the stories about other villages using filtration in Nigeria, the success of Tenu in Tanzania).

- Tell stories which make it clear what specific behaviour needs to happen and shows how it is possible.

Challenging The Environmental Values Of Business Leaders

You'll notice that I am in fact using metaphors here as a way of explaining how activism works. A good example of values conflict over the last fifty years has been the struggle by environmental groups to influence the values of business leaders around the world. Sometimes, their approach has been directly coercive. For example, Weiss, a Hamburg oil refinery, had poured illegal discharge into the harbour for years when Greenpeace activists took the matter into their own hands. They plugged up the pipe and told Weiss they had two hours to work out how to clean up before its tanks started overflowing. The plant shut down for six months during which time it redesigned its processes to produce zero discharge since then (Hawken, Lovins and Lovins, 1999, p 65).

However some environmental activists have taken a completely different approach. Amory Lovins is an example. The Wall Street Journal named him one of 28 people world-wide "most likely to change the course of business". Car Magazine ranked him as one of the 22 most powerful people in the global automotive industry, despite his avowed total opposition to the internal combustion engine. He works with a quarter of the world's top 50 brand names, corporations that he says "are bringing us, at their highest levels, business strategies so radical that you'd think they were written by Greenpeace activists, only more so."

How does Lovins achieve this? He explains "I think this work is attracting more and more adherents across the whole political spectrum and especially in the private sector because it makes sense and makes money. It is quite trans-ideological, and we are of course non-partisan and work with everybody. We are also non-adversarial. We try not to tell people they are wrong; we honor their beliefs as we would our own, even if we disagree with them. This is an art that might be called aikido politics, where you don't fight with an opponent, you dance with a partner. You are committed to process, not outcome, in the belief that from a good process will emerge a better outcome than anyone had in mind in the first place. And then, of course, if that good outcome emerges, as it generally does, your job is to make sure that whoever needs to take credit for it will do so, whether deservedly or not. In the Tao Te Ching there is a remark about water: "That the thing which is of all things most yielding can overcome that which is most hard is a fact known by all but used by none. Being substanceless, it can enter in even where there are no cracks." We need to use the same subtly effective approach in dealing with conflict and diverse ideas about what ought to be done." (Witt, 1999)

Challenging British Rule In India

The most famous historical example of values influencing in international politics was Mahatma Gandhi's campaign to free India from British rule. Gandhi himself was very clear about his own values (Duncan, ed, p 40-64), ranking satya (truth) as his highest criterion, followed closely by non-possession, fearlessness, tolerance, humility and of course ahimsa (non-violence). Gandhi very explicitly used modelling. In fact, the unity of his actions and his beliefs was so total, that when an American reporter asked Gandhi what "message" he had for African Americans in their struggle, Gandhi did not define any principles at all. He simply said "My life is its own message." (Brooks, 1947). Asked another time about his religion, he explained "You must watch my life; how I live, eat, sit, talk, behave in general. The sum total of all those in me is my religion." (Iyer, 1986, p 395).

In March 1922 Mahatma Gandhi faced trial at Ahmedabad for exciting disaffection against the British government and bringing it into hatred or contempt. Examples were given of rioting by people who claimed, however mistakenly, that Gandhi was their inspiration. In response and before sentence was passed, Gandhi made a most eloquent statement which is an excellent example of Values Consulting as taught here. He began with reflective listening: "I would like to state that I entirely endorse the learned Advocate-General's remarks in connection with my humble self.... He is quite right when he says that as a man of responsibility, a man having received a fair share of education, having had a fair share of experience of this world, I should have known the consequences of every one of my acts. I knew that I was playing with fire. I ran the risk, and if I was set free, I would still do the same. I have felt it this morning that I would have failed in my duty, if I did not say what I have said here now. I wanted to avoid violence. Non-violence is the first article of my faith. It is also the last article of my creed. But I had to make my choice. I had either to submit to a system which I considered had done irreparable harm to my country, or incur the risk of the mad fury of my people bursting forth, when they understood the truth from my lips.... I am satisfied that many Englishmen and Indian officials honestly believe that they are administering one of the best systems devised in the world and that India is making steady though slow progress."

Gandhi then went on to present his own case in I message form, concluding "I have endeavoured to give in their briefest outline the reasons for my disaffection. I have no personal ill-will against any single administrator, much less can I have any disaffection towards the King's person. But I hold it to be a virtue to be disaffected towards a government which in its totality has done more harm to India than any previous system.... Holding such a belief, I consider it to be a sin to have affection for the system. And it has been a precious privilege for me to be able to write what I have in the various articles, tendered in evidence against me." (Gandhi, in Duncan, 1972, p 145-150)

Gandhi urged his fellow protestors to remember the essential values shared by both the Christian English government and the Hindu and Moslem Indian population. He considered that these shared values motivated both his protest and his desire to do no harm to the English. He explains "All religions teach that we should live together in love and mutual kindness.... I would appeal to you to let my brethren have its benefit and, as behoves the English people, to defend them, whenever they are maligned." (Gandhi, 1997, p 38).

The Northern Ireland Story

To give you a sense of what influence in a community is like, I want to explain the Northern Ireland story in a little more detail. For many centuries, Ireland (a predominantly Catholic country) was ruled from Britain (predominantly Protestant). Suppression of the Irish population led to the death of over a million people from famine in the 1840s and finally to a 1916 uprising. A treaty with Britain created the Irish Free State in 1921. At that time a substantial majority in the six northern counties of Ireland (most of whom were descendents of British settlers, and most of whom were Protestant by religion) wanted to retain British rule. A separate Northern Ireland state was set up with links to Britain. During the 1960s a civil rights campaign in Northern Ireland protested injustices against the Catholic minority. A British police unit (The Royal Ulster Constabulary) was set up to police civil disturbances (rather brutally, as subsequent investigations have shown) and in 1972 direct rule from London was re-established. The response from the protest movement included the setting up of the paramilitary Provisional Irish Republican Army (IRA) which waged a guerrilla war (or a terrorist campaign, depending on viewpoint) to reunite Northern and Southern Ireland. By the mid 1990s over 3500 people had been killed in community violence and in attacks by the IRA and by "loyalist" Protestant paramilitary groups such as the Ulster Defence Association. The situation seemed utterly insoluble.

In August 1994, after approaches from the governments of Britain and Ireland, the IRA declared a temporary ceasefire and this was reciprocated by loyalist paramilitaries. Peace talks were unable to begin, however, because the British Government of John Major opposed negotiations with pro-IRA political group Sinn Féin until the IRA "decommissioned" all its weapons.

On the urging of the Republic of Ireland, the United States of America now stepped into the situation. In 1995 President Bill Clinton visited Northern Ireland, holding talks with Sinn Féin's Gerry Adams, and Unionist political leaders David Trimble and Ian Paisley. An international mediation team, headed by US Democratic Senator George Mitchell, was set up to begin peace talks in June 1996. His co-facilitators in this process were former Finnish Prime Minister Harri Holkeri and Canadian defence force chief John de Chastelain. In 1997 the Labour Government of Tony Blair took over in Britain. Blair's new attitude to Ireland was demonstrated in his acceptance that decommissioning could run parallel to peace talks, and his historic apology for the British actions in the Irish famine of the 1840s. On Good Friday, April 10th 1998, almost two years after the beginning of the peace talks, they concluded successfully. The resulting agreement was then ratified in a public referendum on 22nd May by 71.12% in Northern Ireland and 94.4% in the Republic of Ireland.

The Northern Ireland Assembly set up by this process survived with former arch rivals Ian Paisley (a unionist) and Martin McGuinness (a former IRA member) in charge. The ceasefire reset in 1998 has held. How did these negotiations succeed where other attempts over the previous thirty years had failed? George Mitchell's description of the process (1999) and the text of the Agreement give some important guidelines which can also be applied in small scale mediation.

George Mitchell's approach has been described by Rushwood Kidder, founder of the Institute for Global Ethics, (Kidder, 1998) as a combination of three elements, described here with Kidder's comments:

- **Patience.** "He listened carefully, kept a low profile, and never gave up."
- **Pressure.** "Mitchell tempered patience with firmness. He set an Easter week deadline and, with unsleeping persistence, compelled the parties to meet it."
- **Principles.** "Amongst the first issues addressed under the heading of "Declaration of Support" were the shared core values upon which the parties agreed.... Build consensus on values, and the relationship can tolerate wide differences at the strategic and operational levels."

Lets review these in relation to the skills we have covered in this book.

Firstly, what Kidder refers to as patience includes clear problem ownership (Mitchell knew that it was the Northern Ireland parties who needed to find solutions, not him) and helping skills (attending, rapport and reflective listening). Mitchell explained that at times he listened through monologues which lasted over two hours, because "I believe in letting people have their say." (Mitchell, 1999, p 86).

Secondly, the "pressure" or firmness is focused on the process of the negotiations, not on the content. Mitchell is not pushing his own solutions, but he is willing to insist on a certain process. He explained "I felt throughout the discussion that ultimately my ability to be effective would depend more upon my gaining the participants' trust and confidence than on the formal description of my authority." (Mitchell, 1999, p 57). Much of the arranging of the process began before the parties even met together. Mitchell met individually with the parties to gather background information, and set out six baseline principles insisting that each party's commitment to abstain from violence was essential to the negotiations. He involved every group from the UDP (the loyalist party supported by the Ulster Defence Association) to Sinn Féin (the republican party supported by the IRA), as well as the British and Irish governments. As negotiations continued, Mitchell's "firmness" involved structuring the process in two main ways:

The talks were set to begin on June 10th 1996. Easter 1998 was set as the ending date because it allowed for a national referendum to be held before the July "marching season" when conflict is more likely between the two conflicting communities. It was also a few days before the British legal basis for the talks as a "Forum" expired. Having a specific time to complete by helped negotiators to shape their comments and keep focused.

The talks had ground-rules and an agenda handed to them by the governments of Britain and Ireland, in June 1996. Marshall was not fooled by this though. He spent the next two months negotiating guidelines and an agenda that were acceptable to the actual participants. The guidelines included a strict confidentiality, and a process for checking "sufficient consensus" (Mitchell, 1999, p 62). This latter essentially allowed any major party to the talks, including the governments of Britain and Ireland, to veto any decision.

Firstly, George Mitchell elegantly guided the various parties to identify some extraordinary shared values as the basis for creating a new Northern Ireland. The Declaration of Support at the beginning of the peace agreement says "We are committed to partnership, equality and mutual respect as the basis of relationships....We reaffirm our total and absolute commitment to exclusively democratic and peaceful means of resolving differences on political issues, and our opposition to any use of threat of force by others for any political purpose, whether in regard to this agreement or otherwise."

Consensus is the name given to the use of win-win conflict resolution in a group. The goal of consensus is a decision consented to by all group members. This doesn't have to mean that everyone thinks this is the very best solution (a unanimous decision). It just means that everyone can live with the decision and will agree to support the group in choosing it. Groups using the method have devised a number of ways to break out of the stalemates which occasionally happen in consensus debates. George Mitchell used these skilfully.

- Vote on whether to accept majority rule for this issue or to continue with consensus. This happened at the very start of the negotiations in 1996, when George Mitchell turned up at the talks with an agenda set by the governments of Britain and Ireland. Although these governments represented the "majority" of human beings on the two islands, other parties at the talks rejected the notion that an agenda could be set in this way and insisted on continuing with a search for consensus even on this "background" issue of the agenda listing.
- Holding smaller "faction meetings" to clarify each party's position. Mitchell used this in mid-1996 when rioting had taken hold of Northern Ireland outside the talks. He explains "It was obvious that no progress could be made in the talks in the current circumstances. But all of the remaining parties wanted the process to continue; they feared that if there were a lengthy adjournment the talks might never resume. I decided that the best approach would be to continue the process but to have the meetings in bilateral form, two or three parties meeting together with the chairman." (Mitchell, 1999, p 60)
- Call a break in the discussion. In early 1997, Mitchell used this method in the middle of a deadlock about the weapons decommissioning process. Sinn Féin were unable to participate in the talks because they refused John Major's demand to decommission *before* discussions. Mitchell said "By early March, it seemed evident that no progress in our negotiations would be possible for a time. ... So on March 5, we adjourned the talks until June. It was a sad and apprehensive leave-taking." During that three month break, the new British government of Tony Blair took office. Suddenly decommissioning while talks were in progress became an option, breaking the deadlock.
- Hold a "Straw Vote" (a test vote) to check the feeling. Mitchell used this process continuously, by meeting with or phoning each party before the

main meetings. At times, he only called the plenary together once he had tested for agreement in this way. This included the final decision on the agreement, which occurred once unionist David Trimble contacted Mitchell to confirm "We're ready to do the business" (Mitchell, p 180).

How George Mitchell Designed His Comments

As mediator George Mitchell's own communication skills were crucial to the success of the talks. Amongst the key skills he needed to demonstrate were:

Reflective Listening and I Messages. Mitchell repeatedly built trust by his ability to state his own opinions and responses clearly, and to listen to and acknowledge others. He did this not only in relation to the technical details of the agreement, but also in relation to the emotional experience of the negotiation process. When faced by an impasse, he says, for example "I told them that I was deeply disappointed and frustrated, as I knew they all were." (Mitchell, 1999, p 127) Mitchell also asked others to use these same skills. This was particularly important at the beginning of the peace talks, when Mitchell said "I made an appeal to all of the participants to moderate their words. I told them that I was familiar with the tactic of demonising one's enemy, having seen it at work in my own country in time of war. This process, however, was not about making war, but about ending war and establishing peace, political stability and reconciliation." (Mitchell, 1999, p 121).

Reframing. a) Meaning: Reframing is skill discussed in an earlier chapter and it has two aspects. Faced by an actual increase in "terrorist" bombings while the Northern Ireland talks struggled forward, Mitchell explained "I think it is becoming increasingly obvious that as the prospect of a successful conclusion of these negotiations improved, those who do not want to see a successful conclusion have taken more drastic and extreme measures." (Mitchell, 1999, p 142). In this statement, Mitchell redefines or "reframes" the increasing violence as backhanded affirmation that the talks are on track. That is a "meaning reframe". The question he had asked himself was "What else could this situation mean, that would be *useful*

Reframing. b) Context: One of the important context reframes that George Mitchell used in Northern Ireland involved accepting that certain statements are useful in certain social contexts. Sometimes, in the public situation of a negotiating room, agreement can be reached more quickly once one party feels that their sense of dignity or identity in their community is safe. At one point in the peace talks, the Sinn Féin newspaper published an interview with an IRA spokesperson. Asked about

Sinn Féin's agreement to put aside violence the IRA spokesperson said "The IRA would have problems with sections of the Mitchell Principles. But then the IRA is not a participant in these talks." (Mitchell, 1999, p 115).

Calls for Sinn Féin to be banned from the talks were immediate. But George Mitchell seems to have recognised that this IRA statement was pitched at more radical sections of the IRA who were still ambivalent about the peace process. In that *context*, the comments were not only understandable, but useful for the peace process. He concluded the resulting debate in the peace talks session with this interesting and multifaceted reframe: "I told them that I understood the never-ending tensions between individual conscience and collective responsibility; between the demands of a constituency and those of the larger society; the simple human conflict between duty to family and duty to public office. For most human beings, I said, life is essentially an endless quest for respect – first self respect, and then the respect of others. There is no surer or more meaningful way to earn that respect than through service to other people. So I told them they would earn the respect of their fellow citizens, and their gratitude, when these negotiations were successfully concluded." (Mitchell, 1999, p 119).

Developing Specific Win-win Agreements. At the end of the process, part of the mediators role is to get written, sensory-specific agreements, which spell out how each party's basic needs or outcomes will be met. In the Northern Ireland case, the agreement involved setting up a North-South Ministerial Council which would connect Ireland (something the republicans wanted) as well as a separate Northern Ireland Assembly (something the unionists wanted). Each group feared that the other would work to make their preferred institution work and sabotage the institution they didn't want. To solve this, the final wording repeatedly included what Tony Blair called a "mutual destruction" clause stating that if one failed, the other would not be able to continue. In real life negotiations, the aim is not always to completely solve all disagreements and leave everyone totally satisfied. In one study on the use of mediation in modern international armed conflict, for example, only 5% of mediations led to settlements, and ceasefires were achieved in 8% of conflicts. However, positive results of mediation were acknowledged by both sides in about 50% of cases (Bercovitch and Rubin, 1992, p 30). The mediation, after all, is one "moment" in an ongoing relationship between the parties. Frequently, as in Northern Ireland, what is arrived at is a "do-able" – a plan that both parties see as meeting some of their concerns better than the status quo, and which advances the sense of cooperation.

Developing this kind of "do-able" agreements is the key pattern that we use in the "Reformer" role, which is the final role used in raising an issue for change (see chapter 3, Social Change Styles and Rapport).

Attitude

An activist's attitude is clearly as important as her or his skills. Science-fiction writer Theodore Sturgeon tells a story about this attitude (much as I like Sturgeon's fiction, this story happens to be true).

One time during Sturgeon's youth, he was at a family gathering with his grandparents and his uncle. His grandfather was a retired English church rector whose 'brains were beginning to melt just a little', while his grandmother was still very much present and 'in charge'. During the gathering, a ferocious argument erupted between Uncle Ernest and the grandmother, about her attempts to make the decisions for the family. The uncle stormed off in a huff, and took an overdose of the adrenaline which he used to counter his asthma. When he came back, he had pinpoint pupils, his cheeks were fiery red, and he held a .38 automatic pistol in his hand. In fury he screamed that he was going to kill himself and burn down the house.

Frantically working out how best to leap into the fray, and simultaneously wondering how his uncle could burn the house down after killing himself, Sturgeon sat on the edge of his chair. Then suddenly, '... my grandfather came back from Out There, set his tea cup down on the low table, got up and stood nose to nose with the wild man. "I say, Ernest", he said in that soft oboe voice of his, "Why can't we all be chums?"'

The effect was dramatic. Uncle Ernest burst into laughter, started coughing, and collapsed into a chair, dropping his gun in the process. The humour in this story is, of course, based on the fact that we all recognise the grandfather's out-of-touch naivety. But Sturgeon offers a dramatic reframe. Who, he asks, is really out of touch with reality? The old man with his simple question: 'Why can't we all be chums?' or those of us who sit powerlessly by as a man plans murder? It is a question which Sturgeon said haunted him every time he watched a couple of cats fighting... or a flight of B52 bombers taking off for some middle eastern village. He concludes: 'So really - why can't we all be chums? Why can't we? Why? It is precisely this question which the activist asks at each moment, to create change.

Summarising Values Influencing

So generally, influencing in a values conflict involves:

1. Finding and utilizing shared values (esp Citizen role)
2. Sharing your opinion in consulting I messages and reflecting (esp Rebel role)
3. Modelling the behaviour you want to be used (esp Change Agent role)
4. Using specific metaphors
5. Reframing challenges as part of finding solutions
6. Creating win-win agreements for practical details without attempting to control the big issues this way. (esp Reformer role)

Creating a Campaign

So you have an issue you want to provoke change about. How do you decide what to do? Here is an overview, regardless of whether you are aiming at change in an organization, community, nation, or planet. Instead of merely reacting to events initiated by power holders, thinking through all these issues will ensure you focus your energy effectively, do not sidetrack or burn out, and have the maximum effect with the least effort. Obviously, if you are in a group, meeting for a prolonged planning session with this kind of checklist would be valuable.

Assessment

A. The Four Roles and the Stages
- What other groups are already active dealing with this issue? Is their approach primarily as Citizens/Rebels/Change-Agents/Reformers?
- Which roles are currently under-expressed, or not positively expressed and which you can most effectively take on yourself?
    o Is someone speaking out about the shared value that is violated?
    o Is someone pointing out that the system itself depends on and protects this violation?
    o Is some group creating a model of the ideal activity that you would like to be available, and documenting it as an alternative?
    o Is someone in a position of power already attempting to create formalised change about this?
- Do people in these various roles conflict or do they understand the value of working together?
- What has happened in the history of this issue already?
- Where are you in the life cycle of a change process?
- What previous setbacks need to be reframed?

B. Choosing a specific goal
- What do you want to happen in 1 year, in 2 years, in 5 years, in 10 years?
- How will you measure the goal being achieved?
- Who in power would need to do what exactly to have it achieved (eg what government agency would need to pass what law) ?

- Does focusing on this goal maximise the image you want to project publically and help feed energy into the next goal if it succeeds?
- How long do you expect to be involved, what time each week do you expect to use, and what money do you expect to use?
- What sources of funding, and sources of information do you need and what do you have access to already?
- What is inspiring about this goal? Can you enjoy the campaign regardless of how long the result takes?
- Under what circumstances would you walk away from the campaign as too difficult for now?

C. Allies

- Who are potential allies once your campaign begins? How can you help them become your allies?
- How will you involve people who become interested in your goal and how will you sustain their support and interest?
- Can you define the issue and goal in a way that is acceptable to everyone you want to be your ally
- How will you handle conflict within your group eg about offers of compromise.

D. Adversaries

- Who benefits from this problem and is likely to try to stop your progress, and what could they do?
- What are your "adversary's" key strengths and weaknesses? What are yours?
- How does your adversary explain to themselves that they are "the good guy"? How can you help them still feel like "the good guy" while changing so you reach your goal?
- Whose cooperation does the current system depend on, and how can that be withdrawn?

E. Tactics

- Which tactics do you have experience of or feel ready to use? (eg online petitions, social media campaigns, vigils, marches, letter writing campaigns, media events, creating media such as videos, magazines, leafleting, door to door canvassing)

Action Stages

1. Citizen Tasks.

- If the issue is new, identify an accepted value or goal in mainstream society that the issue violates and prepare publicity that defends that value and raises the issue as a violation of that value.
- Have clear documented stories of what happens that needs to change to meet that shared value.
- Rehearse consulting statements & prepare reflective listening responses for resistance.

2. Rebel Tasks.
- Begin collecting evidence that the problem is actually deeper than this presenting issue, especially evidence of the way the system, far from fixing the problem, actively defends it.
- Look for trigger events that demonstrate this and confront them, even provoking such events by attempting to stop the problem behaviour or to have people practice non-cooperation with it.
- Prepare for stigmatising of the movement and false flag attacks being blamed on you, as well as actual unhealthy rebel acts by misguided sympathisers.
- Create support systems and positive anchors that can sustain the movement in the "political wilderness".

3. Change Agent Tasks
- Build both a public support movement with powerholders who may be sympathetic, and also a core of activists willing to spend time and take risks exposing the issue publically.
- Find or create structures or groups that can be models of alternative ways of acting that demonstrate the positivity of your goal, and sustain the movement as public interest wanes in the face of slow progress.
- Publicize these models, and build stories of individual examples of successes that can be used as metaphors to inspire society-wide change.
- Plan reframes for the ongoing challenges of the movement and lack of full success.

4. Reformer Tasks
- Get clear as to why minimalist reforms need to be rejected, and what are your bottom lines for compromises and transitional agreements that go some way to meeting the aims without compromising the ongoing movement.
- Identify which people in positions of power can be your voice in advocating reforms that embody your proposal.

Summary

One of the major challenges facing us as social activists is to move beyond pessimism and despair and keep the sense of inspiration that brought us to the movement. NLP is a radical model of personal change with roots in Noam Chomsky's linguistics, and in Alfred Korzybski's studies of linguistic influence. It is based on the "modeling" of how highly successful change agents achieve their results. In this book we looked at how five NLP tools (out of hundreds of such tools) could be used in the service of social change. The five processes are:

Goalsetting:
The most successful goalsetting has eight steps:
Sensory specific. Describe in detail when you will achieve it and what you'll see, hear and feel.
Positive. Focus on what you will get, in positive terms, instead of on the problem situation.
Ecological. Check the other consequences of achieving it.
Choice increasing. Check that it expands your choices rather than narrows them.
Initiated by you. Focus on your actions rather than the responses of the system and others.
First step identified. Understand that several steps may be needed. Do one at a time.
Your resources identified. Creatively use external resources, and inspiring internal meomories.
Feedback. Use all results as feedback to help you decide what to do next.

Social Change Metaprograms and Rapport:
Bill Moyer suggests that there are four key social change roles: Citizen, Rebel, Reformer, and Change Agent. Citizens match and protect mainstream values, and move away from results not aligned with those. Rebels mismatch mainstream systems and push society away from those systems. Change Agents mismatch mainstream systems and move towards and design new systems. Reformers match main-stream systems and move them towards new laws and structures. There are advantages to matching (finding similarity) and mismatching (finding differences). It's also important to know that the basis of successful relationship is rapport, and rapport is built by matching another person's behaviour (eg voice, eye contact, gestures, body position and breathing). There are advantages to both moving away from problems, and moving towards goals. It is also important to notice that moving towards goals is a key to most success, as discussed above.

Reframing:

All social action can be viewed as reframing. In NLP terms there are three main ways to reframe events, all of which depend on the establishment of rapport (discussed above) to succeed. These ways are:
1) Use the "metamodel" questions to invite people back from their current frames to the sensory specific events that they formed their opinions about. This includes challenging presuppositions, mind reads, value judgements, unclear verbs or nouns, and claims of impossibility or necessity.
2) Meaning Reframe. Find a new usefulness for the behaviour or event that the person has a problem with.
3) Context reframing. Find a new context (eg time or place) where the same behaviour or event could be useful.

Anchoring:

Anchoring is a naturally occurring process where one stimulus from one sensory system evokes a full experience including the state of mind that was there in the first contact with the stimulus. This can be used to invite people to step back to a time of relaxation, or of inspiration, or of high energy, re-experience that state whenever they need it, and associate that state with situations where previously they had a problem coping in some way. It can be used to align your various levels of experiencing the challenge. It also works best when you are able to respond resiliently to the situation avoiding the patterns of chronicity such as focusing on why? and what if? questions instead of planning what to do next.

Cooperative Relationships:

The creation of cooperative relationships gives you an essential set of supports for your mission as a change agent. It involving knowing and using skills for four very different situations:

No Problem area: Build positive experiences.	Other Person Owns A Problem: Use Reflective listening.
I Own A Problem: Use sensory specific I messages and listen to the response.	Both Of Us Own A Problem (Conflict). Use the win-win method, or in values conflicts use Consulting and Modelling

We finally focused in on the skills of influencing values and creating conversion or persuasion socially, and noted that, influencing in a values

conflict involves:
1. Finding and utilizing shared values (esp Citizen role)
2. Sharing your opinion in consulting I messages and reflecting (esp Rebel role)
3. Modelling the behaviour you want to be used (esp Change Agent role)
4. Using specific metaphors
5. Reframing challenges as part of finding solutions
6. Creating win-win agreements for practical details without attempting to control the big issues this way. (esp Reformer role)

There's much more of NLP that would be useful for us in the social change situation. My book Transforming Communication gives more background on these five techniques and many others, including an in-depth review of NLP processes for creating a cooperative group, and resolving conflicts. NLP is, as NLP co-developer Robert Dilts says, a model for creating a world that people want to live in. That world has begun already, with you, once you choose to be engaged in this change. The Situationalists said in 1968 in France, that the society that denies creativity makes its own denial the only creative act. I would say even stronger: The society that suppresses love makes its own transformation the most important loving act.

Dr Richard Bolstad is an NLP Master Practitioner and Trainer who has written a number of books on NLP and creating a cooperative world. These include *Creating A Cooperative World, Transforming Communication,* and *Pro-fusion.* He runs New Zealand's largest NLP training company, and trains each year on 5 continents. He also runs world service projects such as training in Sarajevo and the area around Chechnya. He can be contacted at PO Box 35111, Browns Bay, Auckland, phone 09-4784895,   E-mail: learn@transformations.net.nz Website: http://www.transformations.net.nz

Bibliography

Abramovitz, J.N. et alia, Vital Signs 2002 W.W. Norton & Company, New York, 2002

Ackerman, P. and Duvall, J. A Force More Powerful Palgrave, New York, 2000

Alder, H. Think Like A Leader Piatkus, London, 1995

Aldridge, D. "Why are some people healthy and others not? The determinants of health of Populations" in Advances: The Journal Of Mind Body Health, Vol 13, No 4, Fall 1997

Anderson, R.C. Mid-Course Correction Peregrinzilla, Atlanta, Georgia, 1998

Andreas, C. Successful Parenting: An Audio Cassette Program NLP Comprehensive, Boulder, Colorado, 1992

Andreas, S. (2010) Help With Negative Self Talk Real People Press, Moab, Utah

Andreas, S. "What Makes A Good NLPer?" p 3-6 in Anchor Point, Vol 13, No. 10, October 1999

Andreas, S. Virginia Satir: The Patterns of her Magic Science and Behaviour Books, Palo Alto, California, 1991

Ardui, J. and Wrycza, P. "Unravelling Perceptual Positions", in NLP World, Vol. 1, No. 2, 1994, p 5-22

Armstrong, T. The Myth of the ADD Child Penguin, Harmondsworth, England, 1997

Baldwin, A., Kalhoun, J., and Breese, F., "Patterns of Parent Behaviour" in Psychological Monographs, 1945, 58 (3)

Bandler, R. (1985) Using Your Brain For A Change, Real People Press, Moab, Utah

Bandler, R. and Grinder, J. (1975) *The Structure of Magic.* Cupertino, California: Meta Publications

Bandler, R. and Grinder, J. Frogs Into Princes, Real People Press, Moab, Utah, 1979

Bandler, R. and Grinder, J. Reframing, Real People Press, Moab, Utah,

1982

Bandler, R. <u>Magic In Action</u>, Meta Publications, Cupertino, 1984.

Bandler, R., Grinder, J. and Satir, V. <u>Changing With Families</u> Science and Behaviour Books, Palo Alto, California, 1976

Barkley, R. <u>Attention Deficit Hyperactivity Disorder: A handbook For Diagnosis and Treatment</u> Guilford, New York, 1990

Batson, C. D., and Coke, J. S. "Empathy: A source of altruistic motivation for helping?" p 167-187 In Rushton, J.P. and Sorrentino, R.M. (Eds.), <u>Altruism and Helping Behavior</u> Erlbaum, Hillsdale, New Jersey, 1981

Beetham, D. <u>A Beginner's Guide: Democracy</u> Oneworld, Oxford, 2005

Bennett, H.L. and Disbrow, E.A. "Preparing for Surgery and Medical Procedures" p 401-427 in Goleman, D. and Gurin, J. ed <u>Mind-Body Medicine: How to Use Your Mind For Better Health</u> Consumer Reports Books, Yonkers, New York, 1993

Bennett, H.L. Bensen, D.R. and Kuiken, D.A. "Preoperative Instruction for decreased bleeding during spine surgery" in Anesthesiology, No. 65p A245, 1986

Bennis, W. <u>Organising Genius</u> Nicholas Brealey, London, 1997

Bercovitch, J. and Rubin, J. <u>Mediation in International Relations</u> St Martins Press, New York, 1992

Berg, I. K. Family Based Services W.W. Norton & Co., New York, 1994

Bergin, A. and Garfield, S. <u>Handbook of Psychotherapy and Behaviour Change</u>, Wiley & Sons, New York, 1994

Blanchard, K.H. "Ethics In American Business" p 224-233 in <u>New Traditions In Business</u> Berrett-Koehler, San Francisco, 1992

Blumstein, A., Cohen, J. and Nagin, D. eds <u>Deterrence and Incapacitation</u>, National Academy of Sciences Press, Washington DC, 1978

Blumstein, Alfred, Jacqueline Cohen, Jeffrey Roth, and Christy Visher, eds. <u>Criminal Careers and Career Criminals</u> National Academy Press, Washington DC, 1986

Bobes, T. and Bobes, N.S., The Couple Is Telling You What You Need To Know Norton, New York, 2005

Bodenhamer,B.G. and Hall, L.M. <u>Figuring Out People</u> Anglo-American Book Company, Bancyfelin, Wales, 1997

Bolstad, R. "Co-operative Business", in Anchor Point p 31-41 in Vol 15, No 5 (May 2001); and p 4-11 in Vol 15, No 6 (June 2001)

Bolstad, R. (2002) RESOLVE: A New Model of Therapy. Carmarthen, Wales, Crown Publishing

Bolstad, R. (2002) <u>Transforming Communication</u> Pearsons, Auckland

Bolstad, R. (2010) "The How Behind The Secret" Acuity the ANLP Journal, Issue 1

Bolstad, R. and Hamblett, M. "Preventing Violence In Schools: An NLP Solution" p 3-14 in Anchor Point, Vol 14, No. 9, September 2000

Bolstad, R. and Hamblett, M. <u>Transforming Communication</u> Addison-

Wesley-Longman, Auckland, 1998

Bolstad, R. RESOLVE: A New Model Of Therapy Crown House, Bancyfelin, Wales, 2002

Bolstad, R. Transforming Communication Pearsons, Auckland, 2004

Bookchin, M. The Ecology of Freedom Cheshire Books, Palo Alto, California, 1982

Booth, P. Edmund Hillary: The Life of a Legend, Moa Beckett, Auckland, 1992

Bowman, G. "Helping The Blind To See With NLP" p 44-47 in Anchor Point, Vol 10, No. 11, November 1996

Boyett, J. And Boyett, J. The Guru Guide John Wiley & Sons, New York, 1998

Bragg, T. "Resolving Conflict In The Workplace" in Anchor Point, March 1995, p 20-25

Brandenburger, A.M. and Nalebuff, B.J. Co-opetition Doubleday, New York, 1996

Brandon, D. Zen In The Art Of Helping, Dell, New York, 1976

Brockman, W.P. "Empathy revisited: the effects of representational system matching on certain counselling process and outcome variables", Dissertation Abstracts International 41(8), 3421A, College of William and Mary, 167pp., 1980

Brooks, D.J. "Interview with M.K. Gandhi" in The Hindu newspaper, June 15, 1947

Brown, L.R. et alia Vital Signs 2001 W.W.Norton & Co., New York

Bubenzer, D.L. and West, J.D. Counselling Couples Sage Publications, London, 1993

Bureau of Justice Statistics Crime Facts At A Glance U.S. Department of Justice, Washington, 2001 also at: http://www.ojp.usdoj.gov/bjs/glance/

Byrne, R. (2006) The Secret. New York: Atria Books,

Cameron-Bandler, L. Solutions Real People Press, Moab, Utah, 1985

Canfield, J. and Hansen, M.V. A 2nd Helping of Chicken Soup For The Soul. Deerfield Beach, Florida: Health Communications Inc, 1993

Carkhuff, R.R. and Berenson, B.G. Beyond Counselling and Therapy, Holt, Rinehart and Winston, New York, 1977

Carkhuff, R.R. The Art Of Helping Human Resource Development, Amherst, Massachusetts, 1973

Carroll, E. and Mackie, K. International Mediation: The Art of Business Diplomacy Kluwer Law International, The Hague, 2001

Cedar, R. A Meta-analysis of the Parent Effectiveness Training Outcome Research Literature, Ed D. Dissertations, Boston University, 1985

Charvet, S.R. Words That Change Minds Kendall/Hunt, Dubuque, Iowa, 1997

Chevalier, A.J., On The Client's Path, New Harbinger, Oakland,

California, 1995

Chia, M. and Arava, D.A. The Multi-orgasmic Man Harper Collins, San Francisco, 1996

Chia, M. and Chia, M. Healing Love Through The Tao: Cultivating Female Sexual Energy Healing Tao, Huntington, New York, 1986

Chomsky, N. "Rationality/Science" from Z Papers Special Issue, 1995 on line at http://www.zmag.org/chomsky/articles/95-science.html

Chomsky, N. For Reasons of State Vintage Books, New York, 1973

Chomsky, N. Radical Priorities Black Rose Books, Montreal, 1981

Chomsky, N. Syntactic Structures Mounton, The Hague, 1957

Chomsky, N. Understanding Power: The Indispensable Chomsky The New Press, New York, 2002

Chopra, D. The Path To Love Harmony, New York, 1997

Christie, S. and Meltzer, A. The Floodgates of Anarchy Shere Books, London, 1972

Chu, V. The Yin-Yang Butterfly Simon & Schuster, London, 1997

Cialdini, R.B. Influence: Science and Practice Harper Collins College Publishers, New York, 1993

Coddington, D. "Disciplined to Death" p 32-44 in North & South, February 2000

Cohen, A. R. and Bradford, D. L. Influence Without Authority, John Wiley & Sons, New York, 1991

Cohn-Bendit, D. Obsolete Communism: The Left Wing Alternative AK Press, Edinburgh, 2000

Colgan, Dr A. and McGregor, J. Sexual Secrets Alister Taylor Publishers, Martinborough, New Zealand, 1981

Condon, W. S. "Cultural Microrhythms" p 53-76 in Davis, M. (ed) Interactional Rhythms:Periodicity in Communicative Behaviour Human Sciences Press, New York, 1982

Congressional Record, 103rd Congress of the United States of America, Second Session, 1994, S14475, Statement of the President, 6 October 1994

Coover, V., Deacon, E., Esser, C., and Moore, C. Resource Manual For A Living Revolution., New Society Press, Philadelphia, 1978

Covey, S.R. Principle-Centred Leadership Simon & Schuster, New York, 1991

Coyle, J.T. "Psychotropic Drug Use in Very Young Children" Editorial in Journal of the American Medical Association, Vol 283, No. 8, February 23, 2000

Craldell, J.S. "Brief treatment for adult children of alcoholics: Accessing resources for self care"p 510-513 in Psychotherapy, Volume 26, No 4, Winter, 1989

Crum, A.J. and Langer, E.J.,\ (2007) "Mind-Set Matters: Exercise and the Placebo Effect" p 165-171 in *Psychological Science*, Volume 18,

Issue 2, February 2007

Cullen, B. "Two Weeks At Camp David" p 56-61 in Smithsonian magazine, September 2003

Cupertino, 1975.

Dannemann-Kamerman M. "Ecology of Political Systems: Applying NLP To The Understanding of Politics" Series of Articles in The Health Attractor Journal: a) p 14 and 16, Volume 7, Number 2, August 2001; b) p 5, Volume 8, Number 2, August 2002

Dannemann-Kamerman, M. "The Ecology of Political Systems: Making a World to Which People Want to Belong" NLP Comprehensive, http://www.nlpcomprehensive.com/articles/Politics/Politics.htm, 1999

De Bono, E. Sur/Petition: Going Beyond Competition Fontana, London, 1992

Delis, D.C. and Phillips, C. The Passion Paradox Piatkus, London, 1990

DeLozier, J. and Grinder, J. Turtles All The Way Down Grinder, DeLozier and Associates, Bonny Doon, California, 1987

Derks, L., The Social Panorama Model, Son Repro Service BV, Eindhoven, 1998

Derrick, E. Community Development & Social Change Auckland District Council of Social Services, Auckland, New Zealand, 1982

Devaliant, J. Kate Sheppard Penguin, Auckland, 1992

Dewes, K. "Civil Society and Governments as Partners in Nuclear Disarmament", Canadian Network For The Abolition of Nuclear Weapons, March 1998

Dewes, K. and Green, R. "The World Court Project" in Pacifica Review, Vol. 7, No. 2, October-November 1995

Dewes, K. The World Court Project Disarmament & Security Centre, Christchurch, 1998

Dilts, R. and DeLozier, J. Encyclopedia of Systemic Neuro-Linguistic Programming and NLP New Coding, NLP University Press, Scotts Valley, California (Available at http://www.nlpuniversitypress.com/) 2000

Dilts, R. and McDonald, R. Tools Of The Spirit Meta, Capitola, California, 1997

Dilts, R. Changing Belief Systems With NLP Meta Publications, Capitola, California, 1990

Dilts, R. Modelling With NLP Meta Publications, Capitola, California, 1998

Dilts, R. with Bonissone, G. Skills For The Future, Meta Publications, Cupertino, California, 1993

Dilts, R.B., Epstein, T. and Dilts, R.W. (1991) *Tools for Dreamers.* Capitola, California: Meta Publications

Dotz, T., "An Interview With Robert McDonald" in Anchor Point, Vol 12, No. 2, Feb 1998, p 21-30

Dryden, G. and Vos, J. The Learning Revolution Profile Books, Wellington, 1993

Duncan, R., Selected Writings Of Mahatma Gandhi, Fontana, London, 1972

Egan, G. The Skilled Helper Brooks/Cole, Monterey, California, 1975

Egbert, L.D., Battit, G.E. et alia "Reduction of postoperative pain by encouragement and instruction of patients" in New England Journal of Medicine, No. 270 p 825-827, 1964

Elders, F. ed Reflexive Water: The Basic Concerns of Mankind Souvenir Press, 1974

Erickson, M.H. (1980) The Collected Papers of Milton H. Erickson Vol I (ed Rossi, E.L.) Irvington, New York

Erickson, M.H. and Rossi, E.L. Hypnotherapy: An Exploratory Casebook, Irvington, New York, 1979

Ericsson, K. A. (2003) "How the expert-performance approach differs from traditional approaches to expertise in sports: In search of a shared theoretical framework for studying expert performance." In J. Starkes and K. A. Ericsson (Eds.) *Expert performance in sport: Recent advances in research on sport expertise.* (pp. 371-401). Champaign, Illinois : Human Kinetics.

Ericsson, K. A. (2003) "The search for general abilities and basic capacities: Theoretical implications from the modifiability and complexity of mechanisms mediating expert performance" In R. J. Sternberg and E. L. Grigorenko (Eds.) *Perspectives on the psychology of abilities, competencies, and expertise.* (pp. 93-125). Cambridge: Cambridge University Press.

Ericsson, K. A. (2004) "Deliberate practice and the acquisition and maintenance of expert performance in medicine and related domains" in *Academic Medicine.* 10, S1-S12.

Fadiga, L., Fogassi, G., Pavesi, G. and Rizzolatti, G. "Motor Facilitation during action observation: a magnetic stimulation study" p 2608-2611 in Journal of Neurophysiology, No. 73, 1995

Featherstone, L., Henwood, D. and Parenti, C. "Activism: Left Anti-intellectualism and Its Discontents" p 301-314 in Yuen, E., Burton-Rose, D., and Katsiaficas, G. Confronting Capitalism Soft Skull Press, Brooklyn, New York, 2004

Fiedler, F.E. "Factor analysis of psychoanalytic, non-directive and Adlerian therapeutic relationships" p 32-38 in Journal of Consulting Psychology, No. 15, 1951

Finney, J.W. and Moos, R.H. "Psychosocial Treatments for Alcohol Use Disorders" p 156-166, in Nathan, P.E. and Gorman, J.M. A Guide To Treatments That Work, Oxford University Press, New York, 1998

Foner, E. The Story of American Freedom W.W. Norton & Company, New York, 1999

Foner, E. Who Owns History? Hill and Wang, New York, 2002

Franzoi, S.L. Social Psychology Brown & Benchmark, Madison, 1996

Freedman, J.L. "Long term behavioural effects of cognitive dissonance" p 145-155 in Journal of Experimental Social Psychology, Volume 1, 1965

French, M. Beyond Power, Summit Books, New York, 1985

Gandhi, M.K. Hindu Dharma Orient, New Delhi, 1997

Genser-Medlitsch, M. and Schütz, P., "Does Neuro-Linguistic psychotherapy have effect? New Results shown in the extramural section." Martina Genser-Medlitsch and Peter Schütz, ÖTZ-NLP, Vienna, 1997

Goebbels, J. "Jahreswechsel 1939/40. Sylvesteransprache an das deutsche Volk," Die Zeit ohne Beispiel, Zentralverlag der NSDAP, Munich, 1941, pp. 229-239. Published on the Internet in English at http://www.calvin.edu/academic/cas/gpa/goeb21.htm

Goldratt, E.M. The Goal North River Press, Great Barrington, Massachusetts, 1985

Goldratt, E.M. Theory Of Constraints North River Press, Great Barrington, Massachusetts, 1990

Goodkin K., Blancy N.T., Feaster D. et alia (1992) "Active coping style is associated with natural killer cell cytotoxicity in asymptomatic HIV-1 seropositive homosexual men" *Journal of Psychosomatic Research* 1992, 36:635-650

Goodkin K., Blancy N.T., Feaster D. et alia (1992) "Active coping style is associated with natural killer cell cytotoxicity in asymptomatic HIV-1 seropositive homosexual men" *Journal of Psychosomatic Research* 1992, 36:635-650

Gordon, T. "Teaching People To Create Therapeutic Environments" in Suhd, M. M. ed Positive Regard, Science and Behaviour Books, Palo Alto California, 1995, pp 301-336

Gordon, T. Group Centered Leadership: A Way of Releasing The Creative Potential In Groups, Houghton-Mifflin, Boston, 1955

Gordon, T. Leader Effectiveness Training, Peter H. Wyden, New York, 1978

Gordon, T. Parent Effectiveness Training, Peter H. Wyden, New York, 1970

Gordon, T. Teacher Effectiveness Training, Peter H. Wyden, New York, 1974

Gordon, T. Teaching Children Self Discipline At Home And At School, Random House, New York, 1989

Gottman, J.M. and Silver, N. The Seven Principles For Making Marriage Work Three Rivers Press, New York, 1999

Gottman, J.M. The Marriage Clinic W.W. Norton and Co., New York, 1999

Haigh, L. "Empowering Employees: Makes Dollars and Sense" p 7-13 in People and Performance, Vol. 2 No. 2, June 1994

Haley, J. and Hoffman, L. Techniques of Family Therapy basic Books, New York, 1967

Hall, L.M. (2000) "A Few Secrets About Wealth Building" p 25-31 in *Anchor Point journal*, Vol 14, No. 4, April 2000

Handy, C. Beyond Certainty Arrow Books, London, 1996

Hansen, M.V. and Allen, R.G. The One Minute Millionaire Harmony, New York, 2002

Hatfield, E., Cacioppo, J. and Rapson, R. Emotional Contagion Cambridge University Press, Cambridge, 1994

Hawken, P., Lovins, A. and Lovins, L. H. Natural Capitalism Little, Brown and Company, New York, 1999

Haynes, J.M., The Fundamentals of Family Mediation State University of New York, Albany, 1994

Hischke, D. " A definitional and structural investigation of matching perceptual predicates, mismatching perceptual predicates, and Milton-model matching." In Dissertation Abstracts International 49(9) p 4005

Hitler, A. Mein Kampf Houghton Mifflin, Boston, 1943

Hornstein, H. A. Cruelty and Kindness: A new look at aggression and altruism. Prentice-Hall, Englewood Cliffs, New Jersey, 1976

Howard, J.W. and Dawes, R.M. "Linear prediction of marital happiness" p 478-480 of Personality and Social Psychology Bulletin, No 2, 1976

http://www.cartercenter.org/news/publications/health/guinea_worm_public ations/profile-yakubu-gowon.html

http://www.hiv.gov.gy/edocs/rp_ed_radiodramas.pdf

http://www.ihi.org/knowledge/Pages/Measures/default.aspx

Human Security Report http://www.humansecuritybrief.info/figures.html Simon Fraser University, Canada

Ivey, A.E., Bradford Ivey, M., and Simek-Morgan, L. Counseling And Psychotherapy Allyn and Bacon, Boston, 1996

Iyer, R.N. ed The Moral and Political Writings of Mahatma Gandhi Clarendon Press, Oxford, 1986

James, T. "General Model For Behavioural Intervention" in Time Line Therapy® Practitioner Training (manual. Version 3.1), Time Line Therapy™ Association, Honolulu, 1995

Jensen, E.P. Super-Teaching, Turning Point, Del Mar, California, 1988

Kaplan, H. Singer The New Sex Therapy Penguin, Harmondsworth, England, 1974

Kasser, T. and Ryan, R.M. (1996) "Further Examining The American Dream: Differential Correlates Of Intrinsic And Extrinsic Goals" p 280-287 in *Personality and Social Psychology Bulletin*, Vol 22, No. 3, 1996

Kelly, K. New Rules For The New Economy Fourth Estate, London, 1999

Kelly, K. The Secret Of "The Secret". Sydney, Australia: Pan Macmillan, 2007

Kidder, R.M. "Core Values In Northern Ireland" in Ethics Newsline, Institute for Global Ethics, (online at www.globalethics.org/newsline/members/issue.tmpl) April 20, 1998

Kohn, A. Beyond Discipline: From Compliance to Community, Association for Supervision and Curriculum Development, Alexandria, Virginia, 1996

Kohn, A. No Contest: The Case Against Competition,Houghton Mifflin, Boston, 1986

Kohn, A. Punished By Rewards, Houghton Mifflin, Boston, 1993

Kohn, A. The Brighter Side Of Human Nature: Altruism And Empathy In Everyday Life Harper Collins, New York, 1990

Korzybski, A. Science and Sanity, Institute of General Semantics, Englewood, New Jersey, 1994

Kropotkin, P. Mutual Aid: A Factor in Evolution Extending Horizons Books, Boston, 1955 (Original work published 1902)

Laborde, G.Z. Influencing With Integrity Syntony, Palo Alto, California, 1983

Lambert, M. and Bergin, A. "The Effectiveness of Psychotherapy" in Bergin, A. and and Garfield, S. Handbook of Psychotherapy and Behaviour Change Wiley, New York, 1994

Langer, E.J. Mindfulness. Reading, Massachusetts: Addison-Wesley, 1989

LeFevre, D.N. New Games For The Whole Family Perigee, New York, 1988

Legge, J. Chaos Theory and Business Planning Schwartz & Wilkinson, Melbourne, 1990

Lepore, D. and Cohen, Ó. Deming And Goldratt: The Theory Of Constraints And The System Of Profound Knowledge North River Press, Great Barrington, Massachusetts, 1999

Lieberman, S.A. New Traditions: Redefining Celebrations For Today's Family Noonday Press, New York, 1991

Locke, E.A. and Latham, G.P. (1990) "Work Motivation and Satisfaction: Light At The End Of The Tunnel" in Psychological Science 1, p 240-246

Lund, M.S. Preventing Violent Conflicts United States Institute of Peace, Washington, 1996

Lynch, D. And Kordis, P.L. Strategy of the Dolphin Fawcett Columbine, New York, 1988

Macroy, T.D. "Linguistic surface structures in family interaction" in Dissertation Abstracts International, 40 (2) 926-B, Utah State University, 133 pp, Order = 7917967, 1978

Makover, J. Beyond The Bottom Line Simon & Schuster, New York, 1994

Malone, J "Who Needs the Sea Treaty?" p 83 in USA Foreign Policy,

Washington, Spring, 1984

Mann, L., Beswick, G., Allouache, P. and Ivey, M. "Decision workshops for the improvement of decisionmaking: Skills and confidence" in Journal of Counselling and Development, 67, p 478-481, 1989

Manz, C.C. and Sims, H.P. Business Without Bosses John Wiley & Sons, New York, 1995

Marlatt,G. and Gordon, J. Relapse Prevention: Maintenance Strategies in the Treatment of Addictive Behaviours Guilford, New York, 1985

Maruta, M., Colligan, R., Malinchoc, M. and Offord, K. (2000) "Optimists vs. Pessimists: Survival Rate Amongst Medical Patients Over A 30 Year Period" p 140-143 in Mayo Clinic Proceedings, Vol 75; Number 2, February 2000

Maturana, H.R. and Varela, F.J. The Tree Of Knowledge Shambhala, Boston, 1992

McClendon, T. The Wild Days, Meta, Cupertino, California, 1989

McClintock, C. G. "Development of social motives in Anglo-American and Mexican-American children" p 348-354 in Journal of Personality and Social Psychology, No. 29, 1974

McCracken, J. "Creating Cooperative Classrooms" p 48-51 in Trancescript, Number 20, June 2000

McKenna, C. Powerful Communication Skills Career Press, Franklin Lakes, New Jersey, 1998

McMaster, M.D. Performance Management Metamorphous, Portland, Oregon, 1986

McVarish, S. The Greening of New Zealand Random Century, Auckland, 1992

Meece, J.L., Wigfield, A. and Eccles, J.S. "Predictors of Math Anxiety and its Influence on Young Adolescents' Course Enrollment Intentions and Performance in Mathmatics" in Journal of Educational Psychology 82, p 60-70, 1990

Miller, K. Dr Thomas Gordon's Teacher Effectiveness Training Instructor Guide Effectiveness Training, Solana Beach, California, 1994

Miller, S. D., Hubble, M.A. and Duncan, B.L. (1996) Handbook of Solution Focused Brief Therapy, Jossey-Bass, San Francisco

Miller, W. "Motivation for treatment: a review with special emphasis on alcoholism." In Psychological Bulletin, Vol 98 (1), p 84-107, 1985

Mitchell, G.J. Making Peace University of California, Berkeley, Los Angeles, 1999

Monterosso, S., Lyubomirsky, K., White, K. and Lehman, D.R. (2002) "Maximising Versus Satisficing: Happiness Is A Matter Of Choice" p 1178-1197 in Personality and Social Psychology, No 83 (5), 2002

Moore, H.J. "Editors Note for the Web Edition, General Semantics newsletter, Institute of General Semantics, Manchaca, Texas, On the

Internet at http://www.general-semantics.org/library/minteer/pref-01.html

Morris, J. "James Morris on Eric Foner" in Civnet Journal, Vol 3. No. 1, January–February 1999 (on line at http://www.civnet.org/journal/vol3no1/revjmorr.htm)

Moyer, B. with McAllister, J., Finley, M.L. and Soifer, S. Doing Democracy New Society, Gabriola Island, Canada, 2001

Muss, D. "A New Technique For Treating Post-Traumatic Stress Disorder" in British Journal of Clinical Psychology, 30, p 91-92, 1991

Myers, N. Deforestation Rates in Tropical Forests and Their Climatic Implications. Friends of the Earth, London 1989, updated at www.ran.org/info_center/factsheets/04b.html

Mytton, J.A., DiGuiseppi, C., Gough, D.A., Taylor, R.S., and Logan, S. "School-Based Violence Prevention Programs: Systematic Review of Secondary Prevention Trials" p 752-762 in Archives of Pediatric and Adolescent Medicine, 2002, Vol 156, No. 8, August 2002

Nagin, D. "Criminal Deterrence Research at the Outset of the Twenty-First Century" in Tonry, M. ed Crime and Justice: A Review of Research, vol. 23, University of Chicago, Chicago, 1998

Nightingale, E. (2009) "The Strangest Secret" published on line at http://www.innovationtools.com/Articles/SuccessDetails.asp

Nyhart, J.D. and Traintafyllou, M.S. A Pioneer Deep Ocean Mining Venture (Cambridge, Massachusetts Institute of Technology Press, Cambridge, Massachusetts, 1983

Oettingen, G. "Expectancy Effects on Behaviour Depend on Self-Regulatory Thought" p 101-129 in Social Cognition, No. 18, 2000

Oettingen, G. and Gollwitzer, P.M. "Self-Regulation of Goal Pursuit: Turning Hope Thoughts into Behaviour" p 304-307 in Psychological Inquirer, No 13, 2002

Oettingen, G. and Mayer, D. "The Motivating Function of Thinking About The Future: Expectations Versus Fantasies" p 1198-1212 in Journal of Personality and Social Psychology, No. 83, 2002

Oettingen, G. and Wadden, T.A. (1991) "Expectation, Fantasy, and Weight Loss: Is The Impact of Positive Thinking Aways Positive?" p 167-175 in Cognitive Therapy and Research, No. 15, 1991

Oettingen, G. Pak, H. and Schnetter, K. (2001) "Self-Regulation of Goal Setting: Turning Free Fantasies About the Future Into Binding Goals" p 736-753 in Journal of Personality and Social Psychology, No 80, 2001

Patterson, K., Grenny, J., Maxfield, D., McMillan, R. and Switzler, A. "Influencer", McGraw-Hill, New York, 2008

Pavlov, I.P. Conditioned Reflexes: An Account Of The Physiological Activities Of The Cerebral Cortex Oxford University Press, London, 1927

Pennebaker, J.W. and O'Heeron, R.C. "Confiding in others and illness rates among spouses of suicide and accidental death" p 473-476 in Journal of Abnormal Psychology, Volume 93, 1984

Pennebaker, J.W. Opening Up: The Healing Power OF Expressing Emotions Guilford Press, New York, 1997

Perls, F. In And Out Of The Garbage Pail Real People Press, Lafayette, California, 1969

Perls, F.S. Gestalt Therapy Verbatim Real People Press, Moab, Utah, 1969

Pham, L.B. and Taylor, S.E. (1999) "From Thought to Action: Effects of Process Versus Outcome Based Mental Simulations on Performance." P 250-260 in Personality and Social Psychology Bulletin, No. 25, 1999

Phillips, R. Divorce In New Zealand Oxford, Auckland, 1981

Pinker, S. The Better Angels of Our Nature Viking, New York, 2011

Platt, J. "The Skinnerian Revolution" in Wheeler, H. ed, Beyond The Punitive Society, W. H. Freeman & Co., San Fransisco, 1973

Pogrebin, L.C. Family Politics McGraw-Hill, New York, 1983

Prather, H. and Prather, G. I Will Never Leave You Bantam, New York, 1995

Prime Time Productions, The Secret DVD 2006

Prior, R. and O'Connor, J. NLP & Relationships Thorsons, London, 2000

Project Ploughshares http://www.ploughshares.ca/

Reckert, H.W. "Test anxiety... removed by anchoring in just one session?" in Multimind, NLP Aktuell, No 6, November/December 1994

Reiss, A.J., and Roth, J. eds. Understanding and Controlling Violence National Academy Press, Washington DC, 1993

Renesch, J. Ed New Traditions in Business Berrett-Koehler, San Francisco, 1992

Renner, M. Small Arms, Big Impact Worldwatch Publications, Washington, 1997

Rindfleisch, A., Burroughs, J. and Denton, F. "Family Structure, Materialism and Compulsive Consumption," p 312-325 in The Journal of Consumer Research, Vol 23, No. 4, March 1997

Rizzolatti, G., Fadiga, L., Gallese, V. and Fogassi, L. "Premotor cortex and the recognition of motor actions" p 131-141 in Cognitive Brain Research, No. 3, 1996

Rizzolatti,G. and Arbib, M.A. "Language within our grasp" p 188-194 in Trends in Neuroscience, No. 21, 1998

Robbins, A. Unlimited Power Simon & Schuster, London, 1988

Rossi, E.L. ed The Collected Papers of Milton H. Erickson on Hypnosis: Volume IV, Innovative Hypnotherapy, Irvington, New York, 1980

Satir, V. Conjoint Family Therapy Science and Behaviour books, Palo Alto, California, 1967

Satir, V. Peoplemaking, Science and Behaviour, Palo Alto, California,

1972

Satir, V. The New Peoplemaking Science and Behaviour, Mountain View, California, 1988

Schwarz, N., Bless, H., Strack, F., Klumpp, G., Rittenauer-Schatka, H., & Simons, A. (1991). Ease of retrieval as information: Another look at the availability heuristic. Journal of Personality and Social Psychology, Vol 61, No. 2, page 195-202

Scuka, R.F., Relationship Enhancement Therapy Routledge, New York, 2005

Seligman, M.E.P. Learned Optimism Random House, Milsons Point, Sydney, 1997

Seligman, M.E.P. The Optimistic Child Random House, Sydney, 1995

Semler, R., Maverick! Arrow, London, 1994

Senay, I., Albarracín, D. and Noguchi, K. (2010) Motivating goal-directed behavior through introspective self-talk: the role of the interrogative form of simple future tense Psychological Science Vol 21, No. 4: p 499-504, April 2010

Sharp, G. The Politics of Nonviolent Action Porter Sargent Publishers, Boston, 1973

Shaw, G.B. Man And Superman Penguin, Harmondsworth, 1980

Simons, D.J. and Levin, D.T. "Failure to detect changes to people during real-world interaction" p 644 in Psychonomic Bulletin And Review, Vol. 4, 1998

Singhal, A. and Rogers, E.M. "Entertainment Education: A Communication Strategy For Social Change" Lawrence Erlbaum Associates, Mahwah, New Jersey, 1999

Slater, P. Wealth Addiction. Dutton, New York 1980

Slavik, D.J. (2003) "Keeping your eyes on the prize : outcome versus process focused social comparisons and counterfactual thinking" Thesis (Ph. D.), Fayetteville: University of Arkansas

Snow, D.A. and Benford, R.D. "Ideology, Frame Resonance, and Participant Mobilization" p 1997-217 in Klandermans, B., Kriesi, H. and Tarrow, S. From Structure To Action: Social Movement Participation Across Cultures JAI Press, Greenwich, Connecticut, 1988

Solter, A.J. The Aware Baby Shining Star Press, Goleta, California, 1990

Speeter, G. Power: A Repossession Manual University of Massachusetts, Amherst, Massachusetts, 1978

Stephens, G.J., Silbert, L.J. and Hasson, U. "Speaker–listener neural coupling underlies successful communication" in Proceedings of the National Academy of Sciences, June 18, 2010

Sternberg, R.J. "A Triangular Theory of Love" in Psychological Review, 93, p 119-135, 1986

Swack, J.A., "A Study of Initial Response and Reversion Rates of Subjects Treated With The Allergy technique", in Anchor Point, Vol 6, No2, Feb 1992

Sweet, G. The Advantage of Being Useless, Dunmore Press, Palmerston North, New Zealand,1989

Symons, D. The Evolution of Human Sexuality Oxford University, Oxford, 1981

Tanner Pascale, R. Managing On The Edge Simon & Schuster, New York, 1990

Tarrow, S. Power In Movement Cambridge University, Cambridge, 1998

Thalgott, M.R. "Anchoring: A "Cure" For Epy" p 347-352 in Academic Therapy, Volume 21, No 3, January 1986

Thomas, K. "General practice consultations: is there any point in being positive?" in British Medical Journal Vol 294, p 1200-1202, 1987

Thomas, K.B. "The placebo in general practice" p 1066-1067 in Lancet, Vol 344 (8929) October 15, 1994

Timpany, L. (2005) "Building Outcome Bridges" p 3-4 in *Trancescript* Number 36, October 2005

Tonry, M. and Petersilia, J. "Prison Research at the Beginning of the 21st Century" in Tonry, M. and Petersilia, J. Prisons University of Chicago, Chicago, 1999

Ury, W. Getting Past No Century Business, London, 1991

Von Hirsch, A., Bottoms, A.E., Burney, E., and Wikström, P.O. Criminal deterrence and Sentence Severity: An analysis of Recent Research. Hart Publishing. Oxford, 1999

Wall, B. Solum, R. and Sobol, M., The Visionary Leader Prima, Rockman, California, 1992

Wallace, A. and Gancher, D. Eco-Heroes: Twelve Tales Of Environmental Victory, Mercury House, San Francisco, 1993

Walljasper, J., Spayde, J. and the editors of Utne Reader Visionaries New Society Publishers, Gabriola Island, Canada, 2001

Waltman, S.(2006) http://integrationcoach.wordpress.com/2006/08 "Integration Coaching"

Watkins, M. and Rosegrant, S. Breakthrough International Negotiation Jossey-Bass, San Francisco, 2001

Wattles, W. The Science of Getting Rich. Rockford, Illinois: BN Publishing, 2006

Weeks, D., The Eight Essential Steps To Conflict Resolution, G.P. Putnam's Sons, New York, 1992

Wegner, D. "Transactive Memory In Close Relationships" in Journal of Personality and Social Psychology, Vol 61, No. 6, p 923-929, 1991

Weisbord, M.R. ed, Discovering Common Ground, Berret-Koehler, San Francisco, 1992

Wheatley, M.J. Leadership and the New Science Berrett-Koehler, San Francisco, 1994

Whyte, W.F. and Whyte, K.K. Making Mondragon ILR Press, New York, 1991

Wile, D.B. Couples Therapy: A Non-Traditional Approach Wiley, New York, 1992

Williams, J.H.G., Whiten, A., Suddendorf, T. and Perrett,D.I. "Imitation, mirror neurons and autism" p 287-295 in Neuroscience and Biobehavioural Review, No 25, 2001

Williams, P. and Williams, R. How To Be Like Women Of Influence Health Communications Inc., Deerfield Beach, Florida, 2003

Wilson, E. What Is To Be Done About Violence Against Women Penguin, Harmonsworth, England, 1983

Wilson, G.D., and McLaughlin, C. The Science of Love Fusion Press, London, 2001

Wiseman, R. 59 Seconds: Think A Little, Change A Lot. London: Macmillan, 2009

Witt, S. "An Interview With Amory Lovins" E.F.Schumacher Society, 1999, on line at www.smallisbeautiful.org/lovinsinterview.html

Wood, J., Elaine Perunovic, W., & Lee, J. (2009). Positive Self-Statements: Power for Some, Peril for Others. Psychological Science Psychological Science July 1, 2009 vol. 20 No. 7, pages 860-866

Yapko. M., "The Effects of Matching Primary Representational System Predicates on Hypnotic Relaxation." in the American Journal of Clinical Hypnosis, 23, p169-175, 1981

Yuen, E., Burton-Rose, D., and Katsiaficas, G. Confronting Capitalism Soft Skull Press, Brooklyn, New York, 2004

Zeigarnik, A.V. (1927) "Über das behalten von erledigten und unerledigten Handlungen" (The retention of completed and uncompleted actions) p 1-85 in Psychologische Forschung, No. 9, 1927

Zilbergeld, B. The Shrinking of America, Little Brown & Co,Boston, 1983